CELEBRATING
COMMUNITY

God's Gift for Today's World

Edited by
Chris Edmondson and Emma Ineson

DARTON · LONGMAN + TODD

First published in 2006 by
Darton, Longman and Todd Ltd
1 Spencer Court
140–142 Wandsworth High Street
London SW18 4JJ

ISBN-10: ISBN 0–232–52659–1
ISBN-13: ISBN 978–0–232–52659–2

A catalogue record for this book is available from the British Library.

Typeset by YHT Ltd, London
Printed and bound in Great Britain by
The Cromwell Press, Trowbridge, Wiltshire

Contents

Introduction

In our current cultural crisis, the most powerful demonstration of the reality of the gospel is a community embodying the way, the truth and the life of Jesus. Healthy community is the life of Jesus living in us and through us.

Jonathan Campbell quoted in Eddie Gibbs & Ryan Bolger[1]

This quotation comes from a young church leader in Seattle, Washington, and expresses well what is found in so many contemporary books concerned with the future of the Church. At the forefront of the agenda is not just a passing reference to 'community', but the recognition that 'the local church *is* the hermeneutic of the Gospel'.[2] Understanding community living is at the heart of much of the Church's thinking about what it means to be the body of Christ in the world today.

We shouldn't be surprised at this, because in a society that has become fragmented and focused on the individual, their needs and their fulfilment, the recognition is increasingly present that 'It is not good that the man should be alone' (Gen. 1:18). As human beings, we are made for relationship; we are made for community.

There is, as there always has been, something deeply attractive about a group of people who have grasped this vision, who are trying to embody this life and to reflect the image of a God who, in his nature, is community. We see it from the beginning of what we now call 'Church', in that embryonic community that

came into being in first-century Jerusalem, following the day of
Pentecost as described in Acts 2:42–47. There was a group of
people who were 'passionately devoted to God, irrationally
devoted to one another. It was a place where the rich cared for
the poor, where freedom and expectancy marked the worship
and the teaching was transformational. No wonder people were
drawn by and to its life!'[3]

The question that many have asked since then is, 'If this was
possible in first-century Jerusalem, then why not in ...?' Yes, the
context in which we are called to be Church is ever changing,
and it's not naively about replicating things from the first century. Rather, we believe there are core principles laid down there
that sustained the early Church as it was scattered and grew by
persecution, and that can, therefore, inform what it means to be
Church in every generation.

It is no accident that this passage of Scripture has been foun-
dational for so many different expressions of community down
the centuries. What follows in the chapters of this book reflects
that this was the case for the founding and development of the
Lee Abbey Movement which began in Devon in 1946. Our aim in
writing this book is, first, to share with the wider Church some of
the insights and lessons that we have already learned as Lee
Abbey communities. But it is also our conviction that this is a
moment of opportunity when the Church is seeking to rediscover community, a moment for offering models of what it might
mean to be 'mission communities' in today's changing world.
Lee Abbey has a rich history and heritage as a group of Christian
communities, but the aim of this book is not simply to look back
and give ourselves a pat on the back. Our vision is that what is
written here will enable people to make practical connections
into their own lives, churches and ministries, as they seek to
understand how community living might truly be God's gift to
today's world.

There is an increasing realisation that, for Christians, community is not an optional extra, but is God's intention for his
people. Community is not just a new buzz-word. It is not just a

good strategy for church growth, not just a new way of 'doing church', although it may be all of those things. The idea of community has been around for a while. It goes way back beyond the start of Lee Abbey in 1946, for community begins in the heart and the very nature of God, whose 'aim in human history is the creation of an inclusive community of loving persons, with himself included as its primary sustainer and most glorious inhabitant.'[4] The Lee Abbey Movement is a nationwide organisation whose mission and calling is to 'communicate Christ through relationships'. We might say that God has been communicating himself through relationships since the beginning of time. The whole of Scripture tells the story of God creating communities, repeatedly trying to build community with his people, and watching in disappointment as they turn away from him and from his ideas for community living. From Adam and Eve, through Noah, Abraham, Moses, David, Solomon and the prophets, in Jesus and in the early Church, God can be seen striving for community with his people, an ideal which will be fulfilled ultimately only at the end of time when 'God's dwelling is at last with humans'.

It is not surprising that God's priority and purpose throughout history has been building community, because at his very heart, God *is* community, in the nature of the Trinity – Father, Son and Holy Spirit. In Scripture, we see the three persons of the Trinity relating to each other and referring to each other in community and mutuality. Jesus is guided by the Spirit into the wilderness. The Spirit comes in the Son's name and glorifies the Son. The Father says, 'This is my Son, listen to him.' The Son says to the Father, 'Not my will, but yours be done.'

Incredibly, we too are invited to join community with God: 'My prayer is not for them alone. I pray also for those who will believe in me through their message, that all of them may be one, Father, just as you are in me and I am in you. *May they also be in us* so that the world may believe that you have sent me' (John 15:20–21, italics ours). The Lee Abbey vision statement describes joining the community as a 'costly adventure'. For God, the

invitation to us to be in community with him is, and has always
been, a 'costly adventure'. To achieve it, Jesus went to the cross.
There, the perfect unity of the Trinity was torn to let us in, as
Jesus cried out to his Father, 'Why have you forsaken me?' God
is community, but not an exclusive one. Therefore, his people are
called to live openly, to be communities that are not exclusive,
but welcoming and open to others. That is indeed a costly
adventure, as the rest of this book will show.

Looking back down the centuries of Christian history, it seems
that, like the present time, whenever the Church has been at a
'low ebb', some new element 'intervenes' and changes the whole
situation. What is significant is that nearly always, the renewal or
revival that God brings has 'community' at its heart. This was
evident in the third century, when, the Church having become
more 'established' and having lost some of its spiritual fire, the
first expressions of monastic life were born, through St Anthony
and others. Fast forward through St Benedict, St Francis, or in
England the extraordinary 'experiment' in community with
Nicholas Ferrar at Little Gidding, onwards to the nineteenth-
century revival of the 'religious life' in the Anglican Church, to
see a few snapshots of this.

Moving into the twentieth century, following the two great
wars, it seems no coincidence that a cluster of communities in
seemingly very different contexts came into being, born out of
much confusion and struggle in what were dark times. To name
two in particular, through Brother Roger, the Taizé community
was birthed in France, at the same time as the re-establishing of a
community on Iona, both of them seeking to be places of renewal
and reconciliation. Then in 1946, Lee Abbey came into being.

In the late summer of 1945 a number of people had been
consistently praying for a spiritual awakening in the English
Church, in response to Archbishop William Temple's report
Towards the Conversion of England. The vision came to purchase
and establish a centre for training and evangelism. A large house
and estate on the North Devon coast was bought for the grand
sum of £28,000 by a trust overseen by seven men – Cuthbert

Bardsley, Jack Winslow, Geoffrey Rogers, Oswald Garrard, Derek Wigram, Leslie Sutton and Roger de Pemberton. As these men stepped out in faith, purchasing a building for which they did not yet have all the funds, the intention was that the house should be used for Christian house-parties, holidays and training courses. Lee Abbey is now synonymous with community, and yet it is almost by accident that the community exists there at all.

Leslie Sutton was the first acting Warden and as he moved into the house in the winter of 1945, he began to gather around himself Christian men and women who would live at Lee Abbey and fulfil the undertaking with him. Richard More describes in his history of Lee Abbey how these first pioneers of the Movement began to discover that they were embarking on something more than the shared task of running a conference centre; they found they were becoming a community:

> In the winter of 1946–7 those whom God had brought together at Lee Abbey began to work out their relationships, though at that time they knew virtually nothing about community life. Indeed it was almost by accident that they discovered they were a community and had to work out the implications.[5]

Lee Abbey was dedicated as a centre for Christian evangelism on 5 June 1946 and ever since, the people whom God has called to live and work there have been 'working out the implications' of what it means to be a Christian community. In this book, we hope to share some of that 'working out' with the wider Church.

Today, Lee Abbey Devon is run by an international community of about 90 people of all ages who live and work on the 280-acre estate, offering hospitality, rest, activities, worship and teaching to thousands of guests throughout the year. But Lee Abbey is now wider than that first expression of community in North Devon. The calling to 'communicate Christ through relationships' finds expression also in the other parts of the

Movement that have developed since that first community came into being.

In 1964, an International Students' Club was started – a 'home from home' for students studying in London. Up to 150 students from many ethnic backgrounds now live at the Club, which, like Devon, is run by an international Christian community of approximately 40 people.

More recently, Lee Abbey has reached out to provide support and encouragement to individuals, families and churches in some of the inner-city and outer-urban areas of our nation. The Household communities began at Aston in Birmingham in 1988, at Knowle West in Bristol in 1992 and at Blackburn in 1995.

Youth Camps, run by a temporary, dedicated team who form a community for the summer months, have been held in Devon on a field at the bottom of the Lee Abbey estate each summer since 1948. Young people aged between 13 and 25 come to have fun together and to meet God in new ways for a week or two during August.

The latest member of the Movement is the Beacon Youth and Outdoor Activity Centre, which opened in Devon in 2004. The Beacon is a purpose-built centre for adventure holidays, designed with groups of young people and schools in mind.

The Lee Abbey Friends – people around the country who commit themselves to praying for and supporting Lee Abbey – are an essential part of the Movement and have provided vital prayer cover for its work and ministry since it started in 1946.

In Devon, there is a threefold vision, the heart of which has not changed for 60 years: 'to renew and serve the church; to be God's welcome and to build community'. This is, and has been expressed in a number of different ways, in particular through the varied programme in Devon that thousands of individuals and churches appreciate. However, for many guests, the value of a visit to Devon, as with the other parts of the Movement with their different callings, is in becoming in some way a part of an intentional community for a few hours or days.

But just as important as the 'coming' is the 'going', whether that is teams going to work around the country with groups of local churches, or, given the international nature of the communities, the way in which community members often go on to impact the wider Church throughout the world. Over half a million people have been guests at Devon, thousands of students have been part of the London community, and in 60 years, over 5000 people have been community members in the different expressions that make up Lee Abbey. Many people who have come to Lee Abbey over the years have gone away inspired to build community wherever they are. Some have been moved to adapt the Lee Abbey Community Promises that new members make on joining the community (these are printed after this Introduction), to provide a model for shared life and accountability in their own churches or contexts.

Lee Abbey's story so far has been a 'venture of faith'. This seems to be consonant with many other intentional communities that God has called into being. It began, as has been already described, as a gamble, a walk into the unknown. History shows us that it is easy to lose this sense of adventure as a movement becomes a monument and, if we're not careful, ends up as a museum. So far, because of fresh challenges that have been recognised and grasped, the Lee Abbey Movement has something to say to a wider Church that is often deeply conservative and resistant to change.

It seems no accident that the site originally chosen as a centre for evangelism, renewal and training should be literally 'on the edge', in a coastal location where, as the travel brochures have it, 'Exmoor meets the sea'. That seems to be in some sense a parable of where we are meant to be – 'on the edge'. It speaks on the one hand of vulnerability and precariousness, and there is something quite fragile about Lee Abbey. But the 'edge' can also be a place which no one else has explored, a place of excitement and adventure, a place of freedom where the air is fresh – a place from which you can see more clearly. In all its expressions, 'on the edge' seems to be where we are meant to be. This is true for the ministry to guests in Devon, working with students in

London, and alongside churches and communities in challenging parts of our cities in the UK.

At the 2006 celebration weekend marking the first 60 years of Lee Abbey's life and ministry, Paul Bayes, National Mission and Evangelism Adviser for the Church of England, who had not personally encountered Lee Abbey before, said this:

> We can be an anxious and hasty church, running away from our fears and decline. If we are not careful we will rush into initiatives and schemes for growth, with no depth, no reflection, no root in prayer. We talk and talk about 'fresh expressions', and new beginnings, and indeed, God is drawing us there; but we need to know about community and faithfulness, if that talk is to be true, and to bear fruit in changed lives. We are truly facing a 'kairos moment', a moment of God's opportunity ... and your Movement can meet the wider church's 'moment', offering us momentum, to deepen and enrich the changes we are facing.

Our hope and prayer is that the contents of this book, written by people who have been involved in, and shaped by, the 'Lee Abbey experience', will make a contribution to that much-needed momentum.

Chris Edmondson & Emma Ineson
Lee Abbey, June 2006

NOTES

1. Eddie Gibbs & Ryan Bolger, *Emerging Churches* (London, SPCK, 2006).
2. Lesslie Newbigin, italics ours.
3. Bill Hybels from the Willowcreek Community Church, Chicago, speaking at a UK leadership conference.
4. Dallas Willard, quoted in John Ortberg, *Everybody's Normal Till You Get to Know Them* (Zondervan, 2003).
5. Richard More, *The Lee Abbey Story* (Eagle, 1995), p. 36.

The Lee Abbey

Community Promises

Do you affirm before the Community your personal faith in Christ and your desire through prayer, study and service to seek a deep and mature faith?
I do.

Do you understand by this that your mind, your time, your talents, your possessions and all your relationships are to be increasingly surrendered to Christ as Lord?
I do.

Do you promise to be loyal to the Community in its aims, its work, its standards of behaviour, and its disciplines?
I do.

Are you prepared to learn to live in fellowship, being open to be known for who you are, accepting one another in love, and saying of others nothing that could not be said to them personally if love and wisdom required it?
I am.

Have you accepted the discipline of regular private reflection through Bible reading and daily prayer?
I have.

Do you intend to make the weekly Corporate Communion (or, for those looking after children, the Sunday Communion service) the central act of your work and worship?
I do.

Are you ready to serve, in every way, those who come to us, seeking to help one another to a clearer and deeper knowledge of Christ, through your work and by your words?
I am.

1

John Finney

WHY COMMUNITY?

Rt Revd John Finney was Chair of the Lee Abbey Council from 1999 to 2004. He is now retired but was a parish priest for 22 years, then a Diocesan Missioner, an Officer for the Decade of Evangelism and finally Bishop of Pontefract. He headed up the research on how adults come to faith published as Finding Faith Today. *He is co-author of* Saints Alive! *and the* Emmaus *course. His latest book is* Emerging Evangelism *(DLT, 2004).*

[As part of the preparation for this book, 20 people who were involved in Lee Abbey, or who had been fairly recently, filled in a questionnaire, giving their views on living in community. Some were from Devon, and others were from London or the Households. The headline findings of the research are given at the end of this chapter. When referred to, it is called simply 'the Research'. The quotations are taken from the 20 completed questionnaires.]

What is the Lee Abbey 'community'?

'Community' is a notoriously slippery word. That is not surprising, for it covers so much. Head teachers like to call their
school 'a community' – and the word is also applied to a convent
or a village. We have community leaders, community halls and
community policemen, and it is the Community Fund which
dishes out the proceeds of the national lottery. It can be an
Alice in Wonderland 'glory' word which sounds good but has no
content. If there is a common theme, it is the idea of inter-
dependence – it is to do with people acting socially in a way
which is aware of others and accepts diversity. Margaret Betz
provides a useful definition in her book *Making Life Choices*:

> Community is a way of relating to other persons as
> brothers and sisters who share a common origin, a common
> dignity, and a common destiny. Community involves
> learning to live in terms of an interconnected 'we' rather
> than an isolated 'I'.[1]

This is important when thinking of the lessons that Lee Abbey
has to offer us. The interconnected 'we' has many forms, for no
one community is like another. The 35-strong community at the
London Club is very different in context and work to the 100
members of the Devon community. The Club is set in a busy
Kensington street, with Harrods an easy stroll away, while Lee
Abbey in Devon is set in glorious countryside 26 miles from the
nearest supermarket. London serves 150 students who stay for
months, while Devon (in the main house and at the Beacon
Youth and Outdoor Centre) serves over 10,000 guests a year who
each stay for a few days. The Households are different again: two
are in windswept estates, while the Aston Household is in the
heart of a major city. And that is not the end of it, for while the
Households see themselves as a single community, its expression
on the ground varies. Aston is experimenting with a community
living in two houses a few hundred yards apart. Bristol has a
couple living in a smallish three-bedroom semi; Blackburn is one

person living on a housing estate, seeking to be a Christian presence and supporting and being supported by others in the wider community. Thus the Households have three very different sub-communities within their single overarching community.

Besides the three main Lee Abbey communities, there is another which has been called 'the fourth community'. The 3000-plus Friends of Lee Abbey are more than just supporters, and make a real commitment somewhat similar to that of the 'third orders' which can be traced back to St Francis of Assisi. He established three religious orders. The first order were the Franciscan friars. The second order was for nuns. He established this with St Clare – hence their nickname, the Poor Clares. He established yet another order for people who did not live together, called the Third Order of St Francis. Other religious movements, particularly the Dominicans, also have extensive third orders. These may be of particular significance when considering communities, for they do not live in one particular area, but seek to live as Christians wherever they are and support the work of the Church in their own locality. They have a Rule of Life and look to their mother house for refreshment and, often, spiritual guidance, but their primary task is to be Christians in the world. In an internet-connected age in which geography has little significance, this might be the shape of the future.

Thus 'community' has many shapes and cannot be covered simply by talking about being 'in community'. There is no such thing as a single 'Lee Abbey Community'. It is because of this diversity that it has a unique contribution to make to the Church's understanding of community.

Community = commitment

Although the two words sound rather the same, they have different backgrounds. 'Community' stems from the Latin word *communis*, meaning 'common'. When Acts 2:44 says of the early disciples that they 'had all things in common', that succinctly describes some communities. 'Commitment' stems from the Latin *committere*, meaning 'to send together'. It involves a goal, somewhere to aim for together. Community as an end in itself can be introspective, destructive, infantilising. Community for a purpose can be invigorating, strengthening, challenging and exceedingly worthwhile. This purpose can be social, educational, even political.

In the case of Lee Abbey, it is important to note that historically *commitment came before community*. Spurred by the Church of England Report, *Towards the Conversion of England*[2] and buoyed by the success of pre-war house-parties, the original vision was of a centre which would run house-parties in the period from Easter to autumn and provide evangelism training courses during the winter. There was no mention in the early days of 'community'. Those who gave themselves to the task and became the first Trustees saw themselves as a 'team' working together, and the idea of community came a couple of years later. They had long debates as to whether they were primarily 'task orientated' or 'community orientated'. It was argued by some that as the community refined its inner life under the hand of God, so the guests would sense his presence; therefore more should be done to make the life of the community pure and wholesome, and this emphasis should not disappear in a welter of activism. Others thought that God had called the community into being to *do* something and that it was a tool in the hand of God to evangelise and to help the Church to rediscover its mission.

The debate about 'being' and 'doing' has continued down the years, often directed, I suspect, by the personality and spirituality of those involved. Some prefer quietness, space, inwardness, while others want action and a faith which leads to works. In reality both are needed. The life of the community is enormously important, not just in its own right, but as a witness to guests and students. Many visitors comment upon the sense of a God-centred community. But that cannot be all, for there is a task to be done.

Lee Abbey stumbled on community as it did a job. That is the right way round, for as people work together to achieve a goal, so a healthy community is formed. In 2000 I wrote *Fading Splendour?*[3] which examines historically what happens *after* the first wind of the Spirit blows. Usually a group of the like-minded gather together, and often they form a community. It is clear that whenever people gather to form a community just for the sake of being a community, it becomes sick, while if they clearly focus on the goal of serving others, it thrives. This has to be constantly kept in review. The temptation of Lee Abbey down the years, and of many another community, is to put community first and task second. If at Devon the community is ever seen as more important than the guests, or at London as more important than the students, then the vision is becoming faint. The most usual symptom of this is the loss of any sense of perspective. When this happens, the bruises which are inevitable in community life begin to become more significant than the gaping wounds – spiritual, emotional or physical – which the guests and students bring. If the latter are merely seen as the means for supporting the community, then something vital has disappeared. The disciples must often have wanted to stay quietly with Jesus, but he knew he had his Father's work to do. The Mount of Transfiguration has to be followed by the Valley of Confusion.

Jesus said, 'I am among you as one who serves' (Luke 22.27), and each new generation of community members has to be shown the vision and become part of it: otherwise the heady and challenging experience of entering a community swamps the realisation that there is work to be done for the Kingdom.

Members of the community come from many nationalities – at the last count 25 different nations were represented at London and 19 in Devon. This internationalisation of the communities has happened gradually over the years. In the International Students' Club it was obvious from the start in 1964 that there should be non-British people in the community who could more readily relate to the students. In Devon it just happened, greatly to the benefit of all. One London member said she wanted to make connections with both the students and fellow-members of the community and learned to say simple words and greetings in Spanish, Polish, Hungarian, Portuguese, French and Chinese. Those from overseas are not just entering into community, with all the upheaval that entails, but are also encountering a very different culture and a language which most have not met before. It is a mark of God's grace that they do capture the vision and give so richly.

The overall purpose of Lee Abbey is to 'communicate Christ through relationships', with each of the constituent communities translating it into their own context. This operates in two ways. First, there are the internal relationships within the communities. Guests and students often comment on the quality of friendship within the communities in Devon and London, and outsiders feel the warmth from the Households. Often unspoken, the reality of community communicates. The other way is to do with external relationships: friendships are made with guests and others, where Christ is more often communicated through words.

Each of the thousands of people who have contact with the Lee Abbey communities during any particular year should experience *growth*. God will intend for each individual what is right for that person at the time. For one it may be freeing them from bitterness; for another, discovering the beauty of God in Christ; for another, uncovering a gift they never suspected in themselves. Being with Christ as he ministers to them at that precise point is what Lee Abbey is about. The community is to be a tool for God to use.

Next, let us go back to our foundation documents and see what they teach.

Community in the New Testament

The first Christian community was *those who gathered around Jesus*. That has to be the focus of it all. It is too easy for Christian communities to forget this fundamental fact and become more centred upon a particular leader or an ideology or a way of life. Without the hub the wheel will not turn.

This early community may have been a bigger group than we usually assume, for besides the 12 apostles there were the 'many women' who had followed Jesus from Galilee and who 'provided for him' (Matt. 27:55). There were yet more on the edge of the apostolic band – enough to send out 72 'others' on a mission in Luke 10. In Acts 1:15 we hear of 120 who gathered to choose a replacement for Judas Iscariot, and their numbers were quickly augmented as the converts of Pentecost believed and were baptised. They were wonderfully, delightfully close, sharing meals in each other's houses, worshipping together in the temple and rejoicing with all who could say 'Jesus is Lord.' They could not have lived under one roof and sub-groups must have emerged, such as the Jewish 'widows' and those from a Greek background who squabbled in Acts 6:1.

Numbers are important. Ten people in a house group can know each other well. One hundred in a congregation cannot be as close, and 1000 will not even know everyone by sight. Leadership style also has to change. A minister with a congregation of 1000 cannot be as close to them as one with 100. The 12 apostles found in Acts 6 that they needed to adjust their leadership style by delegating as numbers grew, and so does the leadership of any community if it is to survive. Sometimes it has been assumed that the leadership pattern of the Lee Abbey community in London should be the same as that of Devon: it is not, nor should it be – the context and numbers and task are all different.

As the early Church was dispersed into the Mediterranean world by a mixture of persecution and a deliberate policy of mission, 'colonies of heaven' were formed in place after place. In the Epistles we find that there is very little about the 'skeleton' of the body of Christ. Were there bishops? What did a presbyter do? What sort of meetings did they have? What happened at their baptisms? The New Testament does not seem to be particularly interested in these matters that we are so curious about, and over which so much ink and some blood has been spilt. If I may have a moment of heresy: I suspect that there may well have been no overall pattern and each church evolved as best suited its context: a church in rural Asia would have been very different from the one Paul found in the great city of Antioch. In particular, those with a Jewish background in the synagogue would have been different from a church of Greeks whose history had emphasised democracy or a gathering of Romans who tended towards hierarchy and autocracy. Thus any modern attempt to uncover and then copy 'the pattern of the New Testament Church' is bound to fail, for there never was an overall model.

The writers of the Epistles do not seem to have been greatly concerned about the structure of the local body of Christ: they were far more interested in its 'personality' than its 'skeleton'! There are umpteen passages which speak of how Christians are to behave towards each other within the Church: this is true of every strand in the Epistles.[4] These texts speak of the need for unity among those coming from diverse social and spiritual backgrounds, of mutual respect and acceptance, of love needing to abound. At the same time, there were boundaries of behaviour and belief, for certain matters could not be tolerated. The width of these boundaries can surprise us. Paul did not call for those who did not believe in the resurrection to be thrown out of the Church, though he argued strongly that they were wrong.[5] Nor did he even call for the disciplining of those who got drunk at the Lord's Supper, though obviously he abhorred it.[6] He reserved his strongest condemnation for those who tried to restrict the freedom the Christian community had found in Christ. For him salvation meant liberation from a religion of rules as well as from a life of sin,[7] and he longed for that liberation to be seen in the churches he nurtured with such passion and carefulness. All religious communities have to be vigilant against over-regulation. It is right, and inevitable, if people are living closely together, that there should be guidelines as to how they should behave towards each other and how their community should function. However, when these guidelines fossilise into laws and are handed rigidly from one generation to the next, the community turns inwards and becomes more concerned with precise practice than with the love which loosens bonds and yet binds all together.

Questions raised by community

Most communities expect new members to make a commitment to their goals: the newcomer agrees to pursue the same goals as the rest. Traditional religious communities take lifelong vows; Lee Abbey asks new members to make the 'Promises'. This raises two issues which have always to be faced by any community.

Is it essential to live together?

Abbé Paul Couturier spoke of 'the invisible monastery' which 'is made up of all those souls to whom the Holy Spirit has been made known'. He envisaged a common commitment to prayer and Christian living, but not the closeness of living arrangements which characterises a monastery. Any requirement that a community should live together obviously limits its significance, for only a minority can have this privilege. The Third Orders and the experiment of the Households, in being seen as one community but with three different manifestations, are important. The Households have much to teach about the possibility of common commitment without a day-by-day common life. Through other settings such as school, local church and so on we are familiar with the idea of a 'community of belonging'. It can have real power for the Gospel and our own spiritual growth.

Obviously there are disadvantages. There is no doubt that the daily encounter with others means that problems cannot be ducked. Many respondents in the Research spoke of this as one of the most beneficial parts of community life in terms of growth in faith:

being forced to live with people you disagree with ...

life on community[8] is sometimes viewed by those outside
as 'unreal' and somehow an 'easy' option – there are all the
challenges of life outside community but often intensified
because you are living and working together.

But this cannot be for everyone, and the idea of the invisible
monastery, where there is a loose link between those who share a
common vision and a shared commitment, has much power. Jack
Winslow's vision for the Friends had much of this nature, for he
saw Devon as a sort of 'mother house' where Friends would
come to learn more and replenish their energies. A short service
of admission for new Friends emphasises that they are agreeing
not just to support the financial needs of Lee Abbey but also to
'work through prayer and witness for the conversion of others . . .
the renewal of the Church'.

Is it for ever?
In the traditional religious orders, after three years in the pos-
tulancy and the novitiate, a monk or nun will take permanent
vows. These are intended to be lifelong and can only be dis-
pensed with after enormous scrutiny. 'The Order of Mission'
(TOM), founded in 2003 through St Thomas' Sheffield, has the
same pattern: a three-year preparation followed by lifelong
commitment. Lee Abbey has never had such a time requirement
(though the 55 years of Edna Madgwick in Devon far exceeds it!).
Up to the 1980s there was no stipulation as to how long community members should stay, though it was expected that
members would probably leave at some point. Since then there
have been timed contracts: thus the wardens and others in senior
leadership roles have a five-year contract. Community members
may therefore stay for a period which can be as short as a few
months (sometimes this is forced by visa restrictions for overseas
members) or as long as several years, according to individual
circumstances and whether their continued membership of the
community is likely to contribute to their personal development
at all levels.

There are many elements to take into account when deciding how long someone should stay in the community, including their own need for spiritual growth, the health of the whole community, the special gifts they bring, the demands of their wider family and so on. Most of those in the Research knew it was right to leave, however heart-wrenching it was to do so. Months later they reported that they were 'missing the fellowship of the community immensely': 'It was like leaving home for the first time, knowing it was right but at the same time being very hard.'

This has another side to it. Those who remain in the community feel bereft, for at times it seems they are always saying 'good-bye'. The size of the community is a factor: now that the Devon community is around 90 and the average length of stay is about two years, 50 people leave every year – one farewell to be said every week! Nearly all those in the Research spoke of the pain of 'saying good-bye to those you have grown to love and care for'.

When many members of the community leave at the same time, as happens especially in the summer, it can make the community seem like a transit camp, and many in the Research commented on this.

Nevertheless, we have to recognise that in life we generally pass through many communities. Our family is the first, our school the second, the locality where we live a third. We may pass from one church community to another, and yet another. There does seem to be naturalness in this process. Painful though the readjustments which have to be made at each stage may be, they are usually beneficial to our overall development and experience.

In the traditional religious communities, then, one's allegiance is only to the one community and vows are made with that objective. At Lee Abbey there is recognition that there are other communities to which its members rightly belong. They are encouraged to maintain contact with their home church and their family and to keep up to date with developments in the area in which they were trained, so that they can fit back into life once they leave. The Lee Abbey experience should always be seen as transitory, and, in a sense, preparatory for the rest of the person's life.

When this is forgotten there is always the danger of institutionalisation, where someone becomes so comfortable in their niche within the community and their view of the world outside becomes so faint that they flinch from any thought of leaving. Even family ties sink into the background and friendships are formed only with other members of the community. Sadly, when this happens, the tendency is for some regression into adolescence which means that there is a lack of an adult acceptance of responsibility for one's own life and for the environment in which one lives (the true meaning of 'self-control', listed as the last of the fruit of the Spirit in Gal. 5:23).

A summary of the findings from the Questionnaire

In the Research 20 people said what they thought of their time at Lee Abbey. There were 13 responses from present members of community and 7 from past members – enough for a general overview, though not enough for a detailed statistical analysis. One came from a member of the Households, 6 from London and 13 from Devon. Past members included 1 Slovakian, 1 American, 1 Korean and 1 Bolivian. It was noticeable that there seemed to be almost no differences between the London and Devon community members, despite the very dissimilar tasks and context in which they worked: it seems that the experience of being 'on community' was similar for members of both communities.

When asked what they felt was their most important experience of Lee Abbey, nearly all the present members mentioned their own personal development or a new understanding of God. Past members were conscious of valuing the very experience of being part of the community more than those who were still in one: that is, they did not realise its significance until they were no longer part of it.

Benefits

The benefits of being 'on community' that members saw produced a long list (in no particular order and using their own words):

Present members

- 'family atmosphere, great fun'
- 'vitality'
- 'vibrancy and challenge of living alongside so many young people' *(The sheer joy of being part of the fellowship was mentioned by several.)*
- 'sharing and working towards a common vision' *(This was mentioned by many, some of whom compared it favourably with their past Christian experience.)*
- 'the challenge of living with Christians of all denominations and the tolerance this encourages'
- 'having to take other people into account when making decisions' *(Many mentioned that they had learned a greater acceptance of others.)*
- 'sharing life with international people' *(The diversity of the community was mentioned favourably by many.)*
- 'security' *(Some saw this in terms of being in a physically secure place, while others saw it as a safe place in which to experiment.)*
- 'worshipping and praying with those you have spent your week with'
- 'the integration of spiritual and daily life'
- 'explore giftings' *(Several spoke of their surprise in discovering gifts that they had not suspected they had: several spoke of leadership gifts which had been uncovered. One said she was* 'pushed to do things I would not naturally feel able to do, i.e. lead prayers, worshipping in different ways'.*)*
- 'challenging'

Past members

- 'applying biblical principles'
- 'learning to love your neighbour'

- 'deal with conflicts in a different way'
- 'experience different ways of worship and listen to many great teachings and opinions'
- 'how to respect others in a safe environment'
- 'having prayer partners'
- 'not having to put on a mask'
- 'being given the opportunity to serve guests through host teams'
- 'living in a multi-cultural community'
- 'having the support of great friends and pastoral support to help me through some difficult times'
- 'expressing myself freely in big groups'
- 'seeing God in others'

Disadvantages

The disadvantages of being a member of the community also produced a long list:

Present members

- 'temptation to ignore far greater needs outside'
- 'difficult to find space for God'
- 'result in me relying on people rather than God'
- 'need for personal space' (This and 'lack of privacy' was mentioned by almost all.)
- 'turnover. Saying good-bye to those you have grown to love and care for' (Mentioned by half of the respondents.)
- 'there is no escape from unresolved issues' (Advantage or disadvantage?)
- 'hard to become part of existing friendships when you are new'
- 'being let down by others'
- 'difficult to maintain relationships with those outside the community' (Interestingly, one person mentioned the importance of the outside workers: 'they are a connection between ourselves and the "real" world'. This also applied to other parts of their lives: e.g. 'I was out of the housing market'.)

- 'having high expectations of myself'
- 'community has the potential to produce hypocrites'

Past members
  - 'living on the job'
  - 'noise'
  - 'if community is too big one can get lost or unnoticed'
  - 'a little unreal in comparison with the normal world'
  - 'change can take a long time'
  - 'lack of privacy' *(Mentioned by several.)*
  - 'different views on spirituality'
  - 'long hours, especially on host teams, working some 14 hours a day'
  - 'having to say goodbye to close friends regularly'
  - 'I spent the majority of my savings while at LA'
  - 'lack of mental stimulation at work'

Many spoke of the healing they had received – some mentioned physical healing and others healing of their emotions and of the scars of their past experiences:

> I came to Lee Abbey busied and abused, emotionally hurt and significantly wounded spiritually ... God used every opportunity to bring about healing. God not only used the best pastoral people I have had the pleasure to meet and become friends with but also the environment, the people, the animals, and also provided me with the most under-standing doctor I have met.

Without exception, the 20 respondents felt that their Lee Abbey experience was enriching, expanding and exhilarating. They also found it exhausting and deeply challenging. This was particularly significant from those who had left the community and might be expected to have a less positive view in the light of hindsight.

Not one respondent had *not* found the experience beneficial.

Again and again they described their personal development which had taken place during their time in community:

- Lee Abbey provided a 'healthy and safe environment to discover more about yourself and grow spiritually and emotionally'
- 'an environment to grow and take risks'
- 'seeing people as they are and not as I want them to be'
- One just responded in capital letters: 'FUN'.

There were things which they found difficult, but taken overall, their time in community had been immensely worthwhile. It was not just a matter of spiritual growth, though that was mentioned by most. Supremely it was a place for growth as a human being. Someone once described being part of the community as a 'crash course in growing up'. Any adolescent tantrum or sulking or petty self-centredness is soon exposed and has to be faced up to. Any prejudice, whether racial or cultural, or of theological outlook or worship style, is soon challenged when surrounded by people, many of whom are from distant nationalities and who think and react differently from oneself. Above all, there is recognition that there is a work which is being done together – the serving of the guests and students who come to the different parts of Lee Abbey. Some realised that it was all part of a wider vision:

I always saw being at Lee Abbey as a bridge between where I was and where I was going and now recognise this as part of the Lee Abbey vision – refreshing and renewing the church worldwide through community members – what individuals gain from their time of community gets taken into churches and nations.

NOTES

1. Margaret Betz & Doug Fisher (eds), *Making Life Choices* (Paulist Press International, 1992).
2. *Towards the Conversion of England* (Westminster, Press and Publications Board of the Church Assembly, 1945).
3. Darton, Longman and Todd, 2000.
4. E.g. 1 Cor. 3; Heb. 13; Jas. 4; 1 Pet. 4; 1 John 3.
5. 1 Cor. 15.
6. 1 Cor. 1.
7. Cf. the whole of Galatians; Eph. 2:11–22; Col. 6:8–23.
8. Lee Abbey members often speak of their membership of the community as being 'on community'. The use of the word 'on' rather than 'in' may sound strange to outside ears, but over the years it has become an accepted way of referring to the experience of being part of Lee Abbey.

2

David Runcorn

COMMUNITY AND HOSPITALITY

Revd David Runcorn is the Director of Ministry Development for Lichfield Diocese. He was a Chaplain at Lee Abbey Devon for five years and is currently a member of the Lee Abbey Council. He has written on aspects of community and spiritual life in Choice, Desire and the Will of God *(SPCK, 2003) and* Spirituality Workbook *(SPCK, 2006).*

'There is plenty of room for you in my Father's house,' said Jesus. 'I'm on my way to get a room ready for you.'[1] At this point anyone who has ever worked in one of the Lee Abbey communities finds it hard not to picture the risen Jesus ascending to heaven with a duster, polish and a bin liner in one hand and a vacuum cleaner in the other. Preparing to offer hospitality is very hard work.

At the heart of Christian faith is a God who is generously hospitable. In the creation story at the beginning of the Bible he gives his new humanity a beautiful garden to live in (Gen. 2:8 –

probably inspired by ancient Near Eastern 'pleasure gardens'). In the Book of Revelation, at the other end of the Scriptures, brief glimpses into the life of heaven reveal a community of bewildering size and diversity gathered around the throne of God – a community 'that no one could count, from every nation, tribe and language' (Rev. 7:9). This is a place of extraordinary welcome. In his earthly ministry Christ made visible a God who longs to open his life to his world and to welcome the world into his life. So hospitality lies at the heart of the life of God's people. Hospitality and community reveal the character of God like no other activity.

The open door

The ancient world in which the Scriptures originate observed very strict social codes of welcome and hospitality that were honoured across cultural and racial boundaries. To neglect them was to inflict deep insult with very serious consequences. Our Western world has no contemporary equivalent to these. It is very hard for us to imagine the demanding kind of hospitality that was an accepted way of life in the ancient world. The stylised verbal rituals with which Abraham pressed hospitality upon the three strangers who arrived at his tents near Mamre, for example, sound very foreign to our ears (Gen. 18:3ff).

There was practical wisdom in these codes. These were nomadic peoples wandering in a region of harsh and often dangerous terrain. The mutual obligation of hospitality ensured the possibility of refuge, food and refreshment for needy travellers. Next time it could be you.

In today's world the nearest expression of that ancient culture is found among the Bedouin of the Middle East and the Mongolians of central Asia. The Mongolian name for tent is *ger*, the same word as the Hebrew word for 'stranger' or 'alien'.

There is a Mongolian saying that their tents have 'wide doors'. They are places of open welcome. It appals them to learn that a stranger in London has to pay for a cup of tea! The obligation is

laid upon host and guest alike. A traveller must not pass the tent
without stopping to receive its hospitality.

The other fruit of this hospitality was that it provided a way
for strangers to meet. In this way communities crossed boundaries and forged new relationships across racial, cultural and
religious divides.

This culture of hospitality was one very practical factor in
enabling the initial spread of the Gospel in the region. Jesus and
his disciples could depend on it. When Jesus sent the disciples
out on the road, he knew that they would be given somewhere to
stay in the villages they visited, and this was their opportunity to
share, in turn, the hospitality of the love of God (Luke 10:5–7).

Welcoming the stranger

In its teaching on community and hospitality, the Bible builds
upon the social expectations of its time. But it also interprets the
significance of hospitality in strikingly new ways. It was not just
a matter of whether you are hospitable or not. The question is
who you are hospitable to. The test of a hospitable community is
how they welcome strangers and the most vulnerable in society.

There are a number of reasons for this. Firstly, God wills it to
be so. Hospitality and shared life are the heart of God's vision for
humanity made in his image. To be a hospitable community is
most truly to reflect God's likeness and so (incidentally) to be
most truly ourselves. Jean Vanier reflects on this truth from his
experience in the L'arche communities where people of various
disabilities live as equals with the able-bodied. Severely disabled
people have often suffered terrible rejection and are pushed to
the edges of society. Vanier offers a profound and uncomfortable
interpretation of what that behaviour reveals:

> To have cerebral palsy or to be born with severe physical
> handicap ... these are tragic things but they are not the
> most terrible handicap. But to reject such people shows a

deeper sickness. The most terrible disease of all is to have a heart made for love – and not to love.[2]

Secondly, God has a special love for the outsider and the disadvantaged. He has compassion on the needy, vulnerable and powerless. God seeks justice for the orphan and the widow and wants them clothed, fed and cared for. 'If a stranger lives with you in your land, do not molest him. You must count him as one of your own countrymen and love him as yourself' (Lev. 19:33). There are profound issues here in the way our society treats asylum seekers and refugees.

Thirdly, God's people, once established in the land, are to love the stranger because that is what they themselves were once. 'Love the stranger then, for you were strangers in the land of Egypt' (Deut. 10:18–19). One of the less attractive features of human nature is that experiences of struggle and suffering provide no guarantee that we will respond with compassion to others in the same plight. It can be the reverse. We do not like to be reminded. So we tend to reject in others what remains unreconciled within us.

Fourthly, the stranger and wanderer among us is a reminder of our true nature on earth. We too are passing through. We are mortal beings. So the psalmist prays, 'hear my prayer, O Lord and give ear to my cry ... For I am a passing guest, an alien [the word is *ger*], like all my forebears' (Psalm 39:12). In the Letter to the Hebrews the great ancestors of the faith are held up as examples of this. Abraham, Sarah and Jacob 'confessed that they were strangers and foreigners on the earth'. They were 'seeking a homeland' that was yet to be revealed (Heb. 11:13–16).

Reaching out

The model for Christian hospitality is Jesus himself, of course. 'Let the same mind be in you that was in Christ Jesus', says St Paul (Phil. 2:5). What do we learn from him?

Jesus reveals that hospitality requires a willingness to leave home. For him, the supreme expression of hospitality is to journey into the world of another and make it your own. In his earthly life we find him outside any settled patterns of existence or belonging. He had nowhere to lay his head. He lived and died 'outside the city gate' (Heb. 13:13–14), and that is still where his followers must seek him and travel with him. He trained his followers to be wanderers and to travel light (for example, Luke 10:3–4). The first Christians were known as followers of 'The Way'. And now, at the far end of Christian history, where our organisation and ways of doing church have been settled and established for a long time, we are called to rediscover the radical willing exile at the heart of discipleship. We must learn to be travellers once again. When Christians say 'welcome' it is the welcome of a fellow traveller who, with Jesus, has entered into another world and pitched his or her tent there. Simone Weil said, 'We must take into exile the feeling of being at home.'

The New Testament writers borrow more from the language and experience of the exile than any other part of the Old Testament. In fact, the idea of Christians as sojourners or exiles in the world so resonated with their condition that *paroikia* (a place of refuge or exile) became a self-chosen term for a Christian community in any place. So Peter writes his letters to 'the aliens and exiles' (1 Pet. 1:1; 2:11). What is interesting is that this is where the English word 'parish' comes from. How the word has changed! In this land the parish boundaries are the most fixed and permanent signs of belonging. In New Testament times, the words 'parish' and 'parishioner' were understood in terms of leaving home and following Jesus. When Jerusalem was finally destroyed in AD 70, this became a literal exile for many that resulted in the scattering of small communities of faith right across the known world. Within this experience was the call to hope, to pray, to serve and to learn to sing the Lord's song in a land far from home (Ps. 137:4).

From Jesus we learn that hospitality requires a willing self-emptying (Phil. 2:7). The incarnation is the story of the nomadic God who comes into our world as an unrecognised stranger. He was willing to enter our humanity, unacknowledged and as a humble servant. 'The Word became flesh and pitched his tent among us' (the literal translation of 'dwelt among us', John 1:14). So we meet Jesus as a fellow homeless traveller. That is reflected in the approach of Paul as a missionary in the midst of very different cultures. 'To those under the law I became as one under the law, to the Greeks I became as a Greek. I have become all things to all people' (1 Cor. 9:19–23). How would Paul express that same hospitable approach today? It requires a profound and careful costly engagement with worlds and languages unlike our own.

But Jesus' approach to hospitality went much further than the social norms of his day. In many ways it caused more scandal than his teaching. Who he welcomed and whose hospitality he accepted was the problem. It was not just the stranger or the poor whom he welcomed. He accepted meals from tax collectors and welcomed the most morally dubious members of his society into his company. He invited himself to the house of a tax collector. He received anointing from a prostitute and through it he recognised a prophetic sign from God. He touched the leper and accepted the touch of a ritually unclean woman. He loved the unlovely and the unlovable. 'Friend of sinners' remains the most extraordinary name by which Jesus is celebrated. Christian hospitality is not a 'respectable' ministry. It is a way of service and sacrifice. In the humble love of Christ there is no sense of the privileged and powerful 'doing good' to the 'less fortunate' and needy. Jesus came into this world to be its servant. God's love is always beneath our dignity. This hospitality continues to be offered even at the place where it is so terribly rejected. 'He opened wide his arms on the cross.' Even there, in a place where we would only expect judgement and revenge, we are offered a sign of divine welcome.

This is the vision that the Lee Abbey movement has sought to be faithful to. One of the temptations in any community is to settle down, rest on its achievements and just stay at home. And if that home is a beautiful estate on the coast of North Devon, the temptation is stronger than most.

But at its most faithful, the Lee Abbey movement has always been restless. To read its history is to encounter a continuous ferment of ideas and projects. The International Students' Club was one such vision. And, inspired originally by the challenge of the *Faith in the City* report, the Lee Abbey community Households in inner-urban Bristol, Birmingham and Blackburn continue to be pioneering signs of God's hospitality. Alongside these is the continued development of the Devon community and its ministry – most recently the opening of the Beacon Youth and Outdoor Centre and its work among young people.

To go on uprooting and taking its life into exile will be the continuing challenge to the Lee Abbey movement in the search for fresh expressions of Christian witness amidst a culture that is itself so far from home.

Communities without walls

No two communities will express the ministry of hospitality in the same way. Patterns of welcome will be shaped by the specific calling and ministry of each community. But they will have a number of core qualities in common.

Embracing the discipline

The reminder to practise hospitality features regularly in the New Testament teachings. It was a quality particularly looked for in a leader (1 Tim. 3:2) but was also an obligation laid upon the whole community. The writer to the Hebrews encourages the community to continue to show hospitality by reminding them that some 'have entertained angels without knowing it' (Heb. 13:2). I was once welcomed into a remote monastery in Egypt where the guest brother was in the habit of saying, 'We always treat our guests as angels – just in case!'

It is a relief to read that the early Christians found hospitality hard work at times. 'Practise hospitality without complaining', urged Peter (1 Pet. 4:9). It would have been more than just offering Sunday lunch in those days. It would not be booked in advance and could be very inconvenient. Early Christian communities were often among the poorest in their societies. In times of persecution it could even be dangerous. This kind of willing hospitality could be easily exploited.

But if the first Christians were open handed in their welcome, they were not naïve. An early Church teaching manual called *The Didache*[3] offered some very practical guidelines for the ministry of hospitality at the time. It insisted that welcome must be offered to any stranger who turned up. There would be time later for discerning who had come into their midst. But if a prophet or evangelist stays more than three days, they are false teachers. Likewise, if they ask for money, even in a prophetic trance, they are not to be trusted!

Guarding community

A hospitable community will need to take care of the quality of its own life together. Like all Christian ministry, hospitality is demanding. We must learn to say 'no' at times and to close the door. This is what makes real hospitality possible. Without it we become resentful, exhausted and have nothing to offer those who come. For this reason, the Devon community has regular periods in which the house is closed to guests, which enable the community to rest and be restored.

It is neither Christian nor responsible to make ourselves endlessly open to whoever wants us – but this is a common misunderstanding. Self-sacrifice is not the same as self-neglect. Jesus himself was very careful to guard spaces where he could recharge, and he taught his disciples to do the same (Mark 6:31). Hospitality needs the discipline of solitude and withdrawal. If we cannot say no and withdraw at times, then we must ask if all this friendliness may be meeting our own need to be needed rather than reflecting a heart for others. 'Let those who cannot be alone beware of community', is the wise warning of Dietrich Bonhoeffer.[4]

Hospitality to Christ

We more usually speak as if, in welcoming people into our communities, we are welcoming them into the presence of the Christ. By God's grace this may be true, but it is not the whole truth. Jesus more often stresses the reverse. We meet Christ in those who come to us from outside. We meet him in the stranger. Jesus taught that in offering hospitality to strangers and others in need, we are ministering to *him* (Matt. 10:40). 'Whoever receives one such child in my name receives me' (Mark 9:37). He told a disturbing story about the end of time, when people who had apparently been practising a wide variety of Christian ministries were not recognised by Christ because they had neglected hospitality (Matt. 25:31–46). This is the priority Jesus gives to this ministry.

This is one understanding of hospitality that is easily forgotten. It also means that Christian communities and churches should be very cautious in their assumptions about where and among whom Christ will be found. So if we seek the presence of Christ, we must welcome the stranger and the outsider – though it may often seem that Christ has come to us in very heavy disguise! The Rule of St Benedict says:

> All guests who present themselves are to be welcomed as Christ who said, 'I was a stranger and you welcomed me' (Matt. 25:35). The community are to meet them with all the courtesy of love. By a bow of the head or by a complete prostration of the body, Christ is to be adored in them.[5]

The rule of the Taizé community agrees: 'It is Christ himself we receive in a guest. Let us learn to welcome. Let hospitality be *large*' (my italics; literal translation from French).[6]

Out of weakness

Like many others, I joined the Lee Abbey community with a very idealistic view of what living with other Christians would be like. But the demands of shared life are very tough. Jean Vanier comments:

> Community can appear to be a marvellously welcoming and sharing place. But in another way, community is a terrible place. It is the place where our limitations and our egoism are revealed to us. When we begin to live full-time with others, we discover our poverty and our weaknesses, our inability to get on with people, our mental and emotional blocks, our affective and sexual disturbances, our seemingly insatiable desires, our frustrations and jealousies, our hatred and our wish to destroy. While we were alone, we could believe we loved everyone ... In community life we discover our own deepest wound and learn to accept it. So our rebirth can begin. It is from this very wound that we are born.[7]

I recall times when personality clashes and sheer exhaustion meant that love just ran out and no amount of praying seemed to redeem the impulse to strangle that community member who was making my life so miserable. I remember singing the chorus, 'Give thanks with a grateful heart' and getting stuck on one of the lines – 'and now let the weak say, I am strong'. My experience of Christian community at the time was the opposite. I needed to sing, 'and now let the *strong* say, I am *weak*'.

It was the practice at the time to give all new members of the Lee Abbey Devon community a copy of Dietrich Bonhoeffer's book *Life Together*.[8] Bonhoeffer says that we only really become a Christian community when we become communities of the 'undevout'. Initially, and even with the best of intentions, we will try to create this Christian fellowship by sheer will-power. But this is the church of the 'devout' – the Sunday best. It is a self-creation. We will not be able to keep up this image for ever. We come to a point where it runs out. We have nothing more we can give to it.

I recall times when I went into lunch with guests feeling like a complete hypocrite and where parts of community life seemed on the edge of open warfare. The guests never seemed to notice. 'It must be wonderful living here. God is so near. It's so peaceful.' And I would grip the nearest serving slice and think, 'At this moment you're much nearer God than you can imagine!'

It was tempting to be cynical, but I came to realise that it was not any perfection of community that made Lee Abbey the gift it was. It was the willingness to be communities of the *un*devout. We had to lose our idealism and pride. We had to learn to live by grace. God had to do it, not us. And in those times, as we clung onto God and our shared life by our fingertips, a hospitable space seemed to open in our midst where God could invite his guests, be with them and bless them.

Learning hospitality

There is no such thing as a perfect host, actually. Which is just as well, because perfection is not easy company. Hospitability needs to be learned. This is especially true when we are meeting people who are different from us.

'Is there anything you don't eat?' Loving hospitality requires an anticipation of the needs and preferences of others. It is not easy to get it right. We can say 'welcome' but in many other subtle ways we can be communicating the opposite. No one likes the thought that others find us unfriendly. But as someone once observed, 'The last thing we realise about ourselves is our effect.'

I recall one guest describing his arrival at Lee Abbey Devon for a much-needed holiday. The welcome team were waiting enthusiastically. He was greeted warmly. He was welcome! They hoped he would have a restful and refreshing time. But what was actually catching his attention was the large poster pinned to the notice-board immediately behind the receptionist. In big red letters it read: 'GIVE BLOOD'!

In a culture where the great majority of people have no contact with or experience of church or Christian community, offering hospitality is a sensitive task. It requires a lot of listening. There will be a lot of trial and error.

Mr Bean is hysterically funny as he hopelessly fumbles his way through a church service, but what are we to make of this honest response of a woman telling her Christian friend how she felt after attending a church service for the first time?

> You are expecting me to change the way I speak, the sort of music I enjoy, the length of time I usually listen to a speaker, the type of people I mix with, my body temperature, the type of chair I sit on, the type of clothes I am used to seeing people wear, my sense of humour. You expect me to know when to stand, sit and kneel and answer to prayers I have never heard. I am prepared to change but there was nowhere I could connect any part of my life with that service.[9]

Theological hospitality

One unexpected feature of the beginnings of the Lee Abbey movement was its theological inclusiveness. Among the founders there was a conviction that Lee Abbey should include representatives from different traditions of the Church. Those were days when Evangelicalism had yet to emerge from decades of ghetto-like separation from the wider Church and culture. This kind of spiritual and theological hospitality was very pioneering. It took courage and was viewed with considerable suspicion by some.[10]

But so it was that a former USPG missionary and hymn-writer from India, Jack Winslow, joined the Devon community in 1948 as its chaplain. Jack was an Anglo-Catholic by tradition. He already had pioneered an ashram-style of Christian community of mixed race and culture in India. In England he had served on the Archbishop's Commission that produced the report *Towards the Conversion of England*. His influence was enormous. Early walkers looking across the valley to the house could be sure of seeing a light on in his room, where he was known to have his 'hour of contemplative prayer' every morning.

It means that the Lee Abbey movement has, deep in its roots, a loving inclusiveness – theologically and spiritually. It has not always been explicit about this but whenever the movement has strayed into more narrow or excluding expressions of Christian life, an unease would surface somewhere in its midst – a memory or sense that something was being missed that was a distinctive and authentic part of the Gospel character of the movement.

Theological and spiritual hospitality is as important as ever in a Church struggling with sharp disagreements on a number of issues. The Lee Abbey movement, in all its distinct settings, should never underestimate its contribution to the task of thinking out faith across painful tensions, and the struggle for the consecrated mind.

Receptivity and confrontation

Hospitality is not the same as agreeing with people or being endlessly nice to them. I recall my early days as an eager young chaplain at Lee Abbey, going to bed each night with my mouth aching from the effort of smiling at guests and community all day. This had much more to do with my need to be liked than Christian hospitality. But it is not only exhausting to pretend that we agree with everyone around us – it is dishonest.

I remember the moment I began to realise this and the first time that I risked seriously disagreeing with the opinion of a guest at lunch. The conversation suddenly took on a new energy for both of us. It became exciting. On other occasions the attempt to share courteous disagreement brought the conversation to an end. Sometimes it is not a real discussion we want. We are just looking to have our prejudices confirmed.

Henri Nouwen writes that hospitality involves both receptivity and confrontation. Confrontation without receptivity oppresses. It is bullying and leaves people bruised. But receptivity without confrontation is little more than bland niceness. It is actually dishonest and offers nothing. Confrontation is the loving and respectful task of offering ourselves as 'an articulate presence ... showing our ideas, opinions and lifestyle clearly and distinctly'. Hospitality means offering ourselves as a real presence. 'An empty house is not a hospitable house', says Nouwen.[11]

One of the features of contemporary society is how hard it is to find those kind of hospitable places – safe places where real differences can be opened up without immediate judgement and where trust and mutual understanding may become possible.

Reconciliation

For Henri Nouwen, one of the three key movements of the spiritual life was the journey from hostility to hospitality.[12]

We are societies of increasingly fearful separation and isolation. Hospitality easily becomes a means of self-protection. We meet in networks of our own interest groups while hardly knowing the names of our actual neighbours – still less their needs for support and love. We cope less and less well with real differences.

Christian hospitality is called to actively subvert this. This means that hospitality must be expressed on the borders of our society. Hospitality is the offer of a place of real meeting where trust may grow and patterns of fearfulness and hostility may be overcome. It is a bridge-building ministry. It is a ministry of reconciliation. The work of the cross is often spoken of as breaking down or through divisions (e.g. Eph. 2:14).

This was vividly illustrated during the war between Bosnia and Croatia in the early 1990s. The town of Mostar found itself in the front line. The town is named after its ancient stone suspension bridge that crosses the Neretva river as it runs through the rocky gorge below. It was built in 1566 during the reign of Suleiman the Magnificent. Since then, surviving storms and earthquakes, it had provided a vital link between communities separated by that rugged landscape. At 3.30 p.m. on 9 November 1993 it was shelled to destruction by Bosnian artillery. Describing the scene, a reporter quoted this moving Muslim parable:

When Allah, the merciful and Compassionate, first created this world the earth was smooth and even as a finely engraved plate. That displeased the devil who envied this gift of God. And while the earth was still just as it had come from God's hands, damp and soft as unbaked clay, he stole up and scratched the face of God's earth with his nails as much and as deeply as he could. Therefore ... deep rivers and ravines were formed which divided district from district and kept people apart ... And Allah felt pity when he saw what the Accursed One had done ... so he sent his angels to spread their wings over those places and men and women learnt from the angels of God how to build bridges and therefore, after fountains, the greatest blessing is to build a bridge and the greatest sin is to interfere with it ...[13]

Celebration and generosity

When Jesus wanted to illustrate the life in God's Kingdom, he invariably told stories of banquets, wedding feasts and over-the-top celebrations, to which quite unexpected and inappropriate people found themselves invited (e.g. Matt. 22:2–10). His first miracle was to transform a wedding reception where hospitality, in the form of refreshments, had run out (John 2:1–11). But to turn 150 gallons of water into best wine, when guests had 'already drunk their fill' ... that is not just generous, it is irresponsible! When he fed the 5000, he did not simply multiply the meagre offering to provide what was needed. There were 12 baskets of fragments left over (Mark 6:42–43).

Hospitality is often expressed through the gift of a meal, and a special meal is found at the heart of Christian life and worship. In churches anxious to enable outsiders to feel welcome, there is some concern that this meal feels exclusive. But there is a more hospitable way of offering it. One church actually moved its communion table nearer to the entrance of the church to express its welcome and hospitality more clearly.

There is a well-known icon of the Holy Trinity by Andrei

Rublev. It is based on the story of Abraham's hospitality to three strangers who were passing his tent (Gen. 18:3ff). For this reason Christians from the Orthodox tradition will often have this icon on the wall by their front door. In this icon the Father, Son and Holy Spirit are sitting on three sides of a table. There is a deep and gentle reverence in their awareness of each other. The Son and the Spirit are inclining their heads towards the Father. The Father is inclining towards the Son and the Spirit. The table is set for communion and the hand of Jesus is reached out in blessing. There is a beautiful, silent flow of living attentiveness that could almost be a dancing.

But as in all icons, the perspective is inverse. That is to say, the picture opens out towards the watcher. This is deliberate. The picture draws us in and invites our participation. The table has a space kept on our side. What began as a story of human hospitality to strangers is now a picture of divine hospitality towards us. The scene will not be complete until we have taken our place.

I have a print of this icon on the wall where I pray, and my young son joined me early one morning. We began to talk about the scene.

'Do you think they know we are watching them?' I asked. 'What do you think they might say to us? What if they are saying, "Come on, Josh, come on Daddy, join us, we're waiting for you. We can't really start without you!"'

Josh's face broke into a grin at the thought. 'I'll have sausages, beans and chips!' he said emphatically.

NOTES

1. John 14:2. Eugene Petersen, *The Message* (Colorado, NAV Press, 1993).

2. Quoted from a radio broadcast.

3. See *Early Christian Teachings* (Penguin Classics, 1981), *The Didache*, pp. 232–3.

4. Dietrich Bonhoeffer, *Life Together* (London, SCM, 1981), p. 57.

5. Joan Chittister, *The Rule of Benedict – insights for the ages* (New York, Crossroad, 2001), Rule No. 53, 'The reception of guests', pp. 140–4.

6. *Rule of Taizé* (les Presses de Taizé, 1968), p. 115.

7. Jean Vanier, *Community and Growth* (DLT, 1979), p. 5; ch. 6, 'Welcome'.

8. Ibid.

9. Quoted in Richard Giles, *Re-pitching the tent* (Canterbury Press, 1999), p. 58.

10. For further reading see Richard More, *Growing in Faith: The Lee Abbey Story* (Hodder & Stoughton), chs 7 & 10.

11. Henri Nouwen, *Reaching Out* (Fount Paperbacks, 1980), p. 92.

12. Henri Nouwen, *From Hostility to Hospitality*, pp. 61–2.

13. Ivo Andrec, *Bridge over the Drina* (London, Harvill Press, 1995), pp. 208–9.

3

Dave Bookless and
Lucy Larkin

COMMUNITY AND
ENVIRONMENT

Revd Dave Bookless is National Director in the UK for A Rocha, the international Christian environmental organisation, which has a close relationship with Lee Abbey. He has lived in urban, multi-racial Southall since 1991, initially as a vicar, and then pioneering the A Rocha Living Waterways project. He is a contributor to several books, including Caring for Creation *(BRF, 2005).*

Dr Lucy Larkin has a PhD in Environmental Theology. She was a member of the Devon community and now lives in Adelaide, South Australia.

Places can tell powerful stories, and Lee Abbey Devon is no exception. Guarded by the Valley of the Rocks, embraced by ancient hills, buffeted by seas, detailed with ancient woods and pastures, the Lee Abbey estate tells a many-layered story about God, land and people down the centuries. Amongst the many stories of the people who have shaped the land is one which has much to contribute to our theme in this chapter.

A fishy tale

If you walk from Lee Abbey Devon down the road to Lee Bay, you encounter a small river in the valley bottom. Following it uphill, it quickly splits into two streams, the left-hand one running past the lower toll cottage. Several years ago, the then Estate Manager, Jason Hughes, noticed a small sluice gate in this stream, leading off into a mass of marshy overgrown scrub and brambles. Further investigation revealed that the sluice gate fed a series of old fish ponds – covered, unused and silted up through lack of maintenance. It is not clear how old these fish ponds are, but they symbolise a time when the local community managed their environment in a productive yet sustainable way. Feeding today's community and guests is a much larger enterprise, yet fish still have to come from somewhere, and the drastic collapse of North Sea stocks shows how unsustainable much of our current global practice is.

The story of the fish ponds could be used to illustrate how modern consumer society has covered over and forgotten traditional wisdom about our use of the natural world. Later we will look at the poor theology that has allowed Christians – even at Lee Abbey – to be complicit in forgetting our sustainable biblical roots. It is clearly documented that we are living beyond our means, over-consuming at the expense of the world's poor and of future generations. The more we know about the state of the planet, the worse it gets, yet the lifestyle aspirations of our Western democracies paralyse governments from making the necessary radical policy changes. The Millennium Ecosystem Assessment,[1] sponsored by the UN, governments and major scientific institutions, has given us the most comprehensive snapshot ever of the health of planet earth. Water supplies, fertile land, timber and biodiversity are all under severe threat from human activity. Melting ice-caps in Greenland and Antarctica will inexorably lead to massive sea-level rises. Climate change will lead to more frequent, more severe 'natural' disasters, which in reality are deeply unnatural. No wonder experts are worried. Professor John Lawton, outgoing Chief Executive of the National Environment Research Council, described the Millennium Ecosystem Assessment as 'hugely important and profoundly worrying', adding, 'it is difficult not to be profoundly depressed ... we have about fifty years to change things'.[2]

Yet the fish ponds also contain the small-fry of hope. Today undergrowth has been cleared, ponds de-silted, sluices repaired, paths and dipping-platforms added, and the Lee Abbey fish ponds are being used to educate groups of children and young people visiting the main house and the Beacon Youth and Outdoor Centre. Whilst the ponds may no longer be feeding the community, they are feeding the imagination and values of future consumers. It is only as we recognise our total reliance, under God, on the natural world, as we understand that we are stewards, not just shoppers, conservationists, not just consumers, that we can begin to be a people of hope for the world. It may just be that the small groups visiting those long-forgotten fish ponds will cause some ripples to spread much more widely.

Lee Abbey's 'green' history

The story of Lee Abbey and its surroundings over the past 60 years parallels, in many ways, the relationship between Christians and the environment generally. Whilst people have always recognised the beauty of the Devon estate and spoken about its importance, on the whole, creation's central and integral role to all that Lee Abbey stands for has not been given much prominence. Similarly, Christians in Britain have sung happily about God as Creator, whilst failing to see how this relates to our shopping, driving or even evangelism. We have tended to see God as interested only in people, with creation as merely the stage for our activities – an image to which we will return. In doing so, we have been sub-biblical, falling into a human-centred world-view that owes more to Enlightenment humanism than to God's word and Spirit. We have failed to remember that creation is the context for all we are and all we do. We are creatures, created from dust and related to all other creatures. As we shall see, our human relationships in community must be seen in the context of a three-person communal God whose love overflows into a relational creation, of which we are only one part – albeit a key part. We really cannot understand community until we understand our place in creation.

The story of the Lee Abbey community begins with the group of people who were led in prayer to launch out in faith to buy the Devon house and estate in 1945. Lee Abbey's natural setting in God's beautiful creation was crucial to their vision of building a new community of hope in a post-war world. Both Jack Winslow and Leslie Sutton in particular saw God's involvement with the creation as at the heart of all God's dealings with the world. Before World War II, Jack Winslow had been part of an experiment to set up an Anglican Franciscan Community in Pune, India – inspired both by Francis of Assisi's love for all God's creatures, and by the Indian Christian mystic Sadhu Sundar Singh, who, like others before him, believed God spoke both through his word (the Bible) and through his world (creation). Winslow was a poet and hymn-writer, and one of his hymns, still sung today, could have been written with Lee Abbey in mind:

> Lord of Creation, to thee be all praise!
> Most mighty thy working, most wondrous thy ways!
> Who reignest in glory no tongue can e'er tell,
> Yet deign'st in the heart of the humble to dwell.

Leslie Sutton is fondly remembered by John Turner, who first came to Lee Abbey in 1957, six years before Leslie's death. Leslie had invited Lady Eve Balfour, founder of the Soil Association, to visit, and she encouraged Lee Abbey to undertake a full organic conversion. John became Estate Manager with responsibility for all the land and buildings. He speaks of how Leslie 'had a

profound concern for the environment and consciously passed
the mantle on' to him. John also describes how in the 1960s some
had great hopes of Lee Abbey pioneering organic farming and
horticulture as part of its Christian witness:

> The area that is now the car park and Beacon Youth Centre
> was an organic market garden under the supervision of
> Desmond Weir and Ian Geary. There was a conscious
> policy not to use pesticides. Tree planting – especially of the
> beautiful native sessile oaks – was also undertaken as a
> response to shrinking woodland, headed up by Dennis
> Neate, who, after leaving Community in 1971, returned
> each summer for several years to advise on the planting
> programme.

For John Turner, who moved from Devon in 1972, the mantle he
received from Leslie Sutton has sometimes been hard to bear,
since he is no longer part of the community. Over the past 35
years, the early environmental vision has all but disappeared at
times, with the regular change-over of community and council
membership. In every generation there have been those who, to a
greater or lesser degree, kept the light burning – Phil Park and
Bob Purden, to name but two. One, fondly remembered, was
Ursula Kay, former Farm Manager, whose 'Nature Notes' in the
Lee Abbey newsletters summed up what so many love about the
place. Ursula's acute eye, exquisite drawings and combination of
childlike fascination and careful study of the natural world
inspired many. But throughout this time, there was a dislocation
between *passive enjoyment* of creation and *responsible stewardship*
of God's world. Few people made the links between, on the one
hand, beautiful sea views, heart-lifting birdsong and wholesome
Lee Abbey food and, on the other hand, the Torrey Canyon oil
disaster, the poisoning of birds by pesticides, or the indus-
trialisation of farming at the expense of wildlife. For most British
Christians, at Lee Abbey and elsewhere, the environment
was something we took for granted, that gave us unlimited

'resources'. There was little sense of the earth's fragility, of the delicate threads of the web that connect our every action with a reaction somewhere in this finite creation, nor of our complete dependence as creatures upon God's creation. The Lee Abbey estate has often been described as 'God's silent partner', and, in terms of priorities, there have been whole decades in Lee Abbey's history where the noise of human activity has all but squeezed out God's still small voice in creation.

All the world's a stage?

To understand this further, we need to look a bit deeper at how Christians have seen our place on this planet. The image of nature as a stage on which the human–divine relationship is played out has lingered for some time in Christian thinking. If this is our model of reality, the magnitude and urgency of today's ecological crisis demands that we replace it with another, more truthful, humble and workable image for our time. The stage is falling apart and there will be no play without it. God's silent partner is indeed groaning.

Images are powerful; they grasp the imagination and we can live under their sway unconsciously. The trouble with the 'nature-as-a-stage' image is where it places the main players. Humanity is at the centre of attention, God is largely behind the scenes, and the stage itself has merely instrumental value. The image does not adequately express the fullness of our humanity, and it paints a false picture of God – a God who does not relate to the stage itself in any meaningful way. It connects with a troubling aspect of the view of nature as God's 'silent partner' – that the partner can be overlooked or even silenced. Two recent questionnaires amongst community members in Devon and London, undertaken for this book, illustrate this well. The first questionnaire did not mention creation or the estate, and when asked about their 'most important experience at Lee Abbey', only one respondent mentioned the physical setting. However, a second questionnaire asked specifically, 'How significant was the natural beauty of creation around Lee Abbey to you during your time there?' Forty out of forty-two respondents described it as 'crucial' or 'very important' – perhaps illustrating how easily a 'silent partner' can be ignored until attention is drawn to it.

Today, Christian thinkers are suggesting some alternative images that express a more inclusive view than 'nature as stage'. For example, the 'web of life' or 'a community of creatures', or principles such as 'kinship' or 'companionship'. Community itself is a better image. The give and take, inner and outer, suggested by the Lee Abbey logo (see p. xiv) is more expressive of how we are connected to and therefore in relationship with others. To replace the 'nature as stage' image, we need one that understands that relatedness is a reality so fundamental that it is shared by all living beings.

Community, creation and relatedness

Relatedness or relationship is a human condition, an earthly and a cosmic condition and an ethical reality. It characterises religious experience in our longing for deeper relationship with God, and is part of the mystery that is associated with all that exists. By saying that it is a human condition we mean that people exist continually in relationships and feel the joy and the pain that they bring. We are both created within and creators of this relatedness. By relatedness as an earthly and cosmic condition we mean the connection we have with the natural world and the universe. Our bodily existence depends on things of the earth to sustain and feed us. But also we are of the earth, and of particular places such as the ground on which I took my first steps or on which I stand now. So our sense of belonging and thus identity is tied up with the creation.

One of the most evocative images of relatedness we Christians have is the Trinity. The Trinitarian God is a God of relationships. That we can forget God has a relationship with the natural world is a testament to the enduring power of the nature-as-stage model. This is despite the strong theme throughout the Bible and

Christian history of the ongoing relationship between the Creator God and his creatures. It is a central Christian understanding that all things have an enduring creaturely relationship with a Creator, who, whilst being engaged with creation, transcends it.

In the Bible, God is celebrated at the heart of his creation, revealed in its beauty, enabling its fertility and abundance, sustaining this Earth in all its interconnectedness. Psalm 104 and Job 38 are amongst many places where we are reminded of this. Creation is a source of delight to the Creator. God blesses living creatures in their conception, birth, living or dying. This roots all creatures in a physical life that is seen as thoroughly positive and deeply relational. Thus every creature is, in a sense, sacramental; revealing and embodying something of the mystery and diversity of the Creator. As Denis Edwards says in his book *Creation, Humanity, Community*: 'The movement at the heart of cosmic processes does not reach its fulfilment simply in human life or in human history, but only in the embrace between creator and creatures which Christians call grace.'[3]

It is the work of the Holy Spirit to engage with creation, sustaining and empowering it but also bringing about healing. Likewise, Jesus Christ is integral to the cosmic project of healing through his death on the cross and his ushering in of the Kingdom of God. Colossians 1:17 says, 'in him all things hold together'.

This relatedness in the Trinity and between God and the whole universe runs very deep, so that even we humans would not be who we are without our relationships. A person only truly 'comes to be' when in relationship. We receive our being from God, from God's world and from fellow humans. This is not so much a matter of being as of becoming; it is a dynamic process – we continue to be because we are daily sustained by thousands of other beings seen and unseen. The irony is that whilst we saw ourselves strutting on the stage, we were truly static, not allowing ourselves to become fully human, and our spiritual lives missed a dimension that could have made them so much richer. Whenever we neglect our relationship with the stage itself, we can only ever have an impoverished relationship with

God. We miss God revealed in and related to what he has created.

We need new ways to express the truth of our relatedness. We need images that show how we are part of the whole on earth and that this is integral to our Christian lives so that it makes a difference to what we do, the way we live and the way we treat others. It could be said that humanity's place is not centre-stage but created by God as 'response-able' and 'responsible' in an interconnected web – a community – of life.

By *response-able* we mean the ability to respond; that we can relate uniquely to both the environment and to God within the environment. What God says in the rolling hills of Devon is different to what he might say in Lee Abbey's settings in inner-city Birmingham or London or on the Knowle West estate in Bristol or in Blackburn. It is about listening and responding to God in those contexts so that God is not silent. If he could speak audibly, what would he say? Not all parts of nature are lovely. What is he saying in the unlovely aspects of the world? It is about relating to the reality of God in everyday and real contexts. We can also respond to nature itself. Relating to – being rooted in – a particular place teaches us about how to live in and respond to the whole, especially if, as is the case currently, that whole is under enormous stress.

By *responsible* we mean that it is not just about realising that we are in relationship but that we have to do all we can to make our part in the relationship 'right'; in other words, our ethical behaviour. All relating, all relationships are hard. We fail and hurt one another. This is where sin comes in, in the breaking or rupture of relationship. Relationships are marked by sin but also by a calling to be in a certain way – the way of the Kingdom. Thus we know what right relationships are, and that we should do our best to create them. To create right relationship is to take part in the ongoing Kingdom of God. We could say that principles of love, respect, caring, compassion and non-harm should be extended to the estates and the environments in which the Lee Abbey movement is placed.

The shift of perception needed is to extend our understanding of community to all of creation, not just its human counterparts. Living in community includes this dimension, because it is profoundly biblical. As a Christian community, we celebrate the risen Christ at the heart of the cosmic processes. The biblical picture given in Colossians 1:15–20 and Romans 8:22–25 is that the whole cosmos, all things whether on earth or in heaven, are to find reconciliation and right relationship – to find their true community – in the risen Christ. The saving action of God in Jesus is the unfolding of God's purpose in creation, and it is also the beginning of the transformation of all creation.

How do we participate in this transformation? The first step is to recognise that we are interconnected with all others in an earth community, and in fact a cosmic community. The ideal is not the elimination or the domination of other parts of this community, but respect for and commitment to their well-being. When we desire their well-being, we are in a sense desiring our own and God's well-being as well. It makes perfect sense in a relational universe to say that to desire another's well-being is to partici-pate in God's own care for the world. Relatedness in love is of our very essence. We image God in this loving. We participate in God's ongoing Kingdom.

God has created us in such a way that we are radically con-nected to all other matter and to all the forces at work in the universe. We are not merely taking part in a drama of our own making. Rather, humankind is part of the great network of living organisms on this planet. Thus we can affirm a real continuity between human beings and the rest of the living world. We are bodily, connected creatures profoundly interrelated with the rest of creation in our origin, in our present existence, and in God's future for us.

Lee Abbey – living out God's ecology

Our beliefs, our theologies, need to be rooted in the reality of daily life, and Lee Abbey illustrates so much of what has been explored here about community, creation and relatedness. Struggling to live as Christian community in the urban setting of Lee Abbey London or the Households in Bristol, Birmingham and Blackburn serves to illustrate what happens to societies that see nature merely as a stage for human activities.

Martin Ashman, from the Household community at Knowle West, Bristol, says, when he thinks about the environment of his estate, what hits him most is the rubbish, dog litter and chewing-gum. Despite many local government initiatives and projects, there is still a minority of residents who don't care about the environment and make a mess – trees get damaged, paving-stones are ripped up, abandoned bits of bicycles litter the streets. Martin says that there are two men from the council who come and clean his street every working day, but the next day it is dirty again. When we ask why this happens – in Bristol, or in A Rocha UK's urban project in Southall, London – the answers are complex, but ultimately they come back to the same thing. People do not have a sense of connection to, relationship with or responsibility for their local environment. The threads that tie people to place have been broken, and both suffer as a result.

In contexts such as this, what is God saying? To put it another way, what is the Gospel, the 'good news' for areas of urban deprivation? The good news is always about Jesus, and always about transformed, restored relationships. Yet, for A Rocha's 'Living Waterways' project in Southall, the answer has been not simply in words about heaven, but in making a tangible differ-ence to a local environment here on earth. The early Church grew as people saw an expression of community – 'see how these Christians love one another'. In Southall the message has included this, with A Rocha's team living communally (similar to a Lee Abbey Household) in and around a former nursing home in the middle of a multi-racial crime-ridden area. How-ever, the message has tried to go a stage further as well – not just loving each other, but seeing 'how these Christians love their local neighbourhood'. In a modern urban context, many people are so alienated from Church and from the Bible that they need to see God's love demonstrated in tangible ways before they can consider a personal response to the Gospel. So the good news in Southall has included A Rocha acting as the catalyst to transform 90 acres of derelict rubbish-strewn public land into a brand-new country park and nature area.[4] Local children from Sikh, Muslim, Christian and Hindu backgrounds, most of whom start with no idea what a robin or a blackbird look like, are encouraged to join after-school environment clubs and playschemes, to go on nature walks, and even occasionally to 'go wild' through expeditions into the 'scary' countryside beyond the 'safe' city streets. At Lee Abbey's Beacon Centre there are similar stories of young people from areas of urban deprivation, whose first impression of the North Devon woods and hills is one of fear of the unknown – one teenager even asking if there were monkeys on the estate! Through careful leadership and new experiences, many go home with a transformed view of the countryside. It is all about restoring broken relationships – with the creation, with each other, and, ever so slowly, with God as Creator and Saviour.

Back to Lee Abbey, Devon, where creation – whilst silent in human language – shouts aloud of God's glory. Guests and community alike have often described how it is creation that allows them to hear God's voice. Recently, some current and former community members were asked what Lee Abbey's natural surroundings taught them. Some of the responses are worth recording for posterity.

What Lee Abbey's natural surroundings teach me about ...

God

- 'He is majestic, creative and powerful and he speaks loudly or softly through his creation.'
- 'How BIG he is.'
- 'His attention to detail.'

- 'It has made me more aware of God the creator, more in tune with the changing seasons.'
- 'His magnificence, genius, love.'
- 'He is creative, omnipotent, indescribable.'
- 'God loves variety – plants, trees, flowers!'
- 'God's glory, his creativity, his detail.'
- 'The Lord provides. His creativity and wonder.'
- 'The spaciousness of God.'
- 'God's nature, i.e. his greatness, his concern with detail, seasons of life.'
- 'Praise the Lord for his presence in nature.'
- 'How great is the art of God.'
- 'God's peace and beauty.'
- 'God's provision.'

Myself

- 'I am small but significant as a part of his creation.'
- 'My/our responsibility for his creation.'
- 'I'm just small, nothing, but in his hand and part of all.'
- 'A chance to think and listen to God more clearly, SPACE and time to be me with God.'
- 'The contrast between the seasons and the necessity for each – our spiritual lives need all the seasons.'
- 'His care for each and every one of us.'
- 'That God made me with the same care and eye for detail.'
- 'Reminds me that I am finite.'
- 'We are part of nature.'
- 'The God of the whole universe is my father.'
- 'Because we are a part of his creation we are all very special and beautiful.'

Community

- 'As a part of community I have an important role to play in conserving God's creation.'
- 'I'm part of everything.'
- 'God loves variety – he does on [Lee Abbey's] community!'

- 'Personal space is important.'
- 'Walks have been fantastic for getting to know community.'
- 'We are part of creation's community.'
- 'I am grateful for being a part of the community of creation.'

Clearing the brambles

These responses reflect a stream of awareness that has always been present at Lee Abbey, but, like the fish ponds, has sometimes been buried under the brambles of other emphases. In the last few years, though, there has been a spontaneous bubbling up from a number of different sources, all of which feels suspiciously like God's Spirit at work.

Firstly, John Turner was – somewhat to his surprise – invited back to join Lee Abbey Devon's Trustees in the late 1990s. He and his wife Anne were asked to help at a week in 2000 when Dave Bookless of A Rocha,[5] the Christian practical conservation organisation, was speaking. In turn, Dave had been invited at the suggestion of another key individual – James Pender – a former volunteer at A Rocha Portugal, who then joined the Estate team. Whilst on a walk across Exmoor, John Turner mused to Dave, 'Wouldn't it be wonderful if there could be some kind of alliance between A Rocha and Lee Abbey?' Things moved on slowly, and in 2004 John Turner took some environmental papers up to a Council meeting in London, with the hope of speaking to the new Chairman, Bishop John Perry. However, the day was too full with other matters, and John returned home feeling very discouraged, but that evening there was a phone call from Dave Bookless – four years after they had met at Lee Abbey! They felt the time was now right to move forward, and John wrote to John Perry, who agreed to put it on the agenda of the next meeting. When the meeting came, it was extraordinary how one person after another said that they had links with A Rocha. Chris Edmondson, as Warden in Devon, joked, 'Is there any way to get to heaven except by being a member of A Rocha?' As the laugh went around the room John Turner said it was like the Holy

Spirit breathing through that meeting. The decision was taken unanimously that representatives of Lee Abbey and A Rocha should explore ways to work more closely together. In April 2005 an agreement was signed, designed to ensure that a practical concern for God's creation is preserved as an integral part of the whole Lee Abbey movement, as well as bringing the benefits of Lee Abbey's long experience of community into A Rocha.

Meanwhile, God was at work elsewhere too. In 2004 Jonathan Woolven was appointed as the new Estate Manager for Lee Abbey Devon. He writes:

> I saw seminars advertised at New Wine by Dave Bookless of A Rocha. I was no great conservationist but something told me I ought to go to these. The two sessions totally changed my views of conservation, and the Biblical perspective was taught to us – our duty in this area made quite clear. The timing was so clearly of God.

Soon after Jonathan arrived at Lee Abbey he spoke to John Turner, and he describes the meeting:

> His mouth fell open as I told him of my hopes and plans. They were very similar to those he had had as Estate Manager some 40 years earlier. But little came of these. The time was probably not right then as it was so far from the culture of the day.

Jonathan was also given a dream, a vision of the Lee Abbey estate 'feeding body, mind and spirit'. He writes:

> I was amazed some weeks later to read similar words used some years earlier. It was revealed to me that in 'body' the estate could exhibit sustainable farming and in 'mind' it could be used to teach our responsibility to God for conservation of his creation. In 'spirit' we are to maintain a setting in which people can draw closer to God by

witnessing the continuing gift of his beautiful and abundant creation.

Another stream bubbled up in the form of Lucy and Jonathan Larkin, associated with Lee Abbey for some time, involved with the Knowle West Household, and also passionate Christian environmentalists. They had no idea of the other developments, but Lucy, possessing a PhD in Eco-theology, wrote a paper on 'Why Lee Abbey should go green', and, with Jonathan being a qualified environmental consultant, they offered to undertake an 'Environmental Audit' of Lee Abbey Devon. This all happened quite spontaneously and independently – and it was only in November 2004 that the Larkins, John Turner, Jonathan Woolven and Dave Bookless met together as a group for the first time.

The small-fry of hope

As Lee Abbey looks back on 60 years of God's leading, and looks forward for God's direction into the future, the role of the natural environment needs to move from the shadows into greater prominence. The 'silent partner' is groaning too loudly to be ignored, and our role as priests of creation is to voice its pain, and work with God for its recovery. Just as Lee Abbey's old fish ponds, with which we began, are now being re-used to bring about a new relationship between young people and nature, so the Lee Abbey movement can have a role to play in renewal. Lee Abbey can be an example both to the wider Church, and to a society desperately in need of ecological hope. We now have the opportunity to integrate care for God's creation into the heart of the Lee Abbey movement. Care for creation not as an 'optional add-on' dependent on the enthusiasm of a few individuals, but at the heart of Lee Abbey's understanding of community. It needs to be in the DNA of Lee Abbey to examine and reduce its own environmental footprint – in Devon, London or the Households, and indeed, in the Friends' groups around the country. It needs to be integral to Lee Abbey's sense of calling to renew the Church in its relationship with creation. This will not happen without hard work and sacrifice, and the current signs of hope in the movement are still small and vulnerable, but hope is such a rare commodity today that they are worth nurturing and building upon.

In July 2004, Archbishop Rowan Williams gave a keynote speech on Christianity and the environment, entitled 'Changing the Myths we live by'. In it he stated:

> It seems the moment to look for a new level of public ser-
> iousness about environmental issues. And the Church's
> contribution has to consist not primarily or exclusively in
> public lobbying, though that is important, but in its
> showing forth ... the truth of creation's relation with the
> creator and especially the role of human work and thought
> within that.

Lee Abbey is a place where that truth can be shown forth – incarnated – in relationships between God, people and nature – and in prophetically challenging the wider Church to follow.

This book could aptly be sub-titled 'Living together in a world falling apart'. We have already mentioned Colossians 1:17 where Jesus is described as the one 'in whom all things hold together'. The flip-side of this is that Jesus is also the one without whom all things fall apart. The falling apart that we are seeing around us – spiritually, socially and ecologically – is ultimately the result of failing to acknowledge the Lordship of Jesus over every area of his creation. For this, all of us need to repent. At Lee Abbey we need to admit to God the occasions when we have allowed God's creation to be merely peripheral to our work: the times when the focus has been on people alone rather than the full scope of God's purposes; the times when decisions about food, energy, buildings or transport have failed to include our response to God as stewards of creation; the times when the Devon estate has been seen only in strictly commercial terms, as a 'resource' rather than as God's property on loan – a precious gift held in trust.

More positively, the rediscovery of a truly biblical notion of community – including God, people and the whole created order – allows us to work with God in rebuilding where the world is falling apart – again spiritually, socially and ecologically. Lee Abbey's great strength over the last 60 years has been in the first two of these dimensions. Spiritually, countless people have been reborn and renewed as individuals. Socially, in the melting-pot of community living, numerous relationships have been healed, past hurts faced, even churches reconciled. But how about ecologically? Lee Abbey communities should be places that enable thousands to be restored and released in their relationship with God's world. Visiting Lee Abbey Devon gives the opportunity to take time apart from the busyness, rush and materialism of modern life – time to reconnect with our creatureliness, to renew our sense of awe and wonder, and to rediscover the relationships and rhythms that God wants us to live by. Peter Harris, founder and International Director of A Rocha, talks of 'the GM church, where the DNA of our societies has been patched in such a way that the Gospel we preach is no longer biblical', because it is so tainted by the idolatry of individualism and materialism. Just as the founders of Lee Abbey in post-war Britain saw this as a place where a broken society could be renewed in Christ, so today there is an opportunity for a new vision for the twenty-first century – a vision of Lee Abbey as a community of people who live and share a Christ-centred hope for the planet. This is a *kairos* moment for God's Church to recover our very first human calling – to 'tend and keep the garden' of God's creation. There is no more timely calling today.

NOTES

1. See www.millenniumassessment.org – where all the documents and evidence can be studied or downloaded.
2. Transcribed verbatim from Sir John Lawton's speech at the MEA's launch (London, Royal Society, 31 March 2005).
3. Denis Edwards, *Creation, Humanity, Community* (Gill & Macmillan, 1992), p. 58.

4. A video about this project, *A New Creation – Living Waterways in the Urban Desert*, is available for £10 from A Rocha UK, 13 Avenue Road, Southall UB1 3BL.

5. A Rocha ('The Rock' in Portuguese) has grown from one project in Portugal and now works in 15 countries across 5 continents. See www.arocha.org.

4

Emma Ineson

COMMUNITY AND
WORSHIP

*Revd Dr Emma Ineson was a Chaplain at Lee Abbey Devon from 2003
to 2006, following a job-share curacy with her husband Mat. Her
doctoral research was a study of the nature of power and authority in
the language of worship.*

Whether in the beautiful Octagonal Lounge in Devon, in the
chapel in Kensington, London, in a rainswept tent on a soggy
camp field, tucked in the broom-cupboard of a semi in Blackburn, in a living-room in Knowle West in Bristol, or in a church
in the multi-faith area of Aston, Birmingham, you will find a
different expression of worship authentic to Lee Abbey.

The Lee Abbey movement has been involved throughout its
history in developing new and creative ways of worshipping.
The exploration of experimental liturgies and worship patterns
means community members are inspired to 'push the boundaries' in worship, whilst remaining true to valuable and meaningful traditions. It has been part of the vision to encourage and

enable the local church in achievable, authentic and exciting worship. The Lee Abbey movement is Anglican in foundation but is ecumenical in the members that make up its communities and is becoming increasingly international. A range of church-manship was represented amongst the early founding members of Lee Abbey in Devon (for example, Jack Winslow was Anglo-Catholic, Leslie Sutton was Evangelical). More recently, an even greater variety has been represented. The London and Devon communities are made up of over 20 different nationalities and many denominations, including Romanian Brethren, German Lutheran, Polish Roman Catholic, British Anglican and South American Pentecostal, to name but a few.

As the wider Church engages with new ways of being which 'surprise and delight, and yet ring true with the past' (to quote David Ford), we will want to be asking: What is the role of corporate worship – both in the life of the Church community and in reaching out to those as yet outside the Church?

In post-Christian Britain the challenge to the Church today is to reach out to a society disillusioned with, and cynical about, institutional religion. The concept of community, of fellowship, of relationship is something many are searching for. But many also yearn for a sense of 'the other', transcendence, meaning, experience. Immanence and transcendence are both found in Christian worship at its best.

Worship builds community

The reason we worship is first and foremost to give God his worth.[1] But worship also forms and builds community. Worship enables community to grow and vice versa: 'May the God who gives endurance and encouragement give you a spirit of unity among yourselves as you follow Christ Jesus, so that with one heart and mouth you may glorify the God and Father of our Lord Jesus Christ' (Rom. 15:5).

Many of St Paul's instructions to the early Church about the way corporate worship is conducted are to do with protecting and maintaining relationships in the Church family. Anything that affects the good functioning of the body, including disorder or disrespect in worship, is condemned.[2]

Worship and community are inextricably linked. The way a community worships reveals who it is as well as what it believes God to be like. Henri Nouwen describes prayer and worship as 'the realization of God's presence in the midst of his people and, therefore, the realization of the community itself'.[3] Corporate worship is the place where the values of a community are expressed most clearly – in the way in which they lay out their worship space, in what they provide as a visual focus, in the music they use, in the way they greet each other (and new-comers), in what they pray about, in their choice of Scripture readings and preaching and in how they celebrate holy communion.

Jesus said to 'do this in remembrance' of him. The trouble is, he didn't tell us *exactly* what to do or *exactly* how to do it. And so, wherever two or three are gathered in his name, they will do it differently from the two or three gathered down the road.

Worship, and particularly a weekly sharing of holy communion, is the central point of community life for Lee Abbey. As Dietrich Bonhoeffer says in his classic book on community, *Life Together*: 'The fellowship of the Lord's supper is the superlative fulfilment of Christian fellowship ... Here the community has reached its goal. Here joy in Christ and his community is complete.'[4] Corporate worship, and particularly holy communion, builds unity in the community: 'As we eat and drink these holy gifts, make us one in Christ, our risen Lord'.[5]

That makes it all sound very easy. Anyone who has lived and worshipped in community will know that it doesn't always feel like a time of 'superlative fulfilment'! And yet it remains the central part of community life. When community members have been at Lee Abbey for approximately three months, they are asked to make three promises. One of them is: 'Do you intend to make the weekly Corporate Communion the central act of your work and worship?'

The weekly act of breaking bread together is central to all that we are and all that we do, the pivot around which the rest of life and work revolves and from which it is fed and resourced. It is significant that the weekly communion at Lee Abbey Devon is called 'Corpus' – the Latin word for 'the body'.

This strong expression of unity highlights all the more the pain that is evident when parts of Christ's body are not able to share together in bread and wine. David Bainbridge, the Warden of Lee Abbey London, tells of an application to join community from a woman in the Russian Orthodox Church. After prolonged correspondence it was decided that it did not feel right to invite her to join the community, as her church would not permit her to share communion outside the Orthodox Church and she would not therefore be able to share in that 'central act of work and worship' with the rest of the community. This decision was painful on both sides, with all feeling the pain of divided churches. More recently, a Hungarian Roman Catholic woman joined community, apparently accepting the expectation that she would share in communion with the community. On arrival, however, she felt she could not take the bread and wine, and for some weeks held back and was clearly uncomfortable. Eventually it was agreed that she should come forward for a blessing, and so participate as fully as she could under the circumstances. This restored the sense of unity and mutual respect. David says:

> I think now that, if we have another applicant from the Russian Orthodox Church, then we should accept the pain of divided Christendom into the community, welcome the applicant as a non-Communicant member of community, and see this as a small step towards the unity of the Spirit which we all long for.[6]

A shared life

Working is a significant part of the vocation to community. When people join the community in Devon they are allocated to a different work team: house, kitchen, estate, administration, pastoral, youth and so on. Much of the work that is done is far more basic than people's qualifications and abilities have prepared them for. Those scrubbing pans, pruning trees and cleaning toilets might have university degrees and years of experience in their professional field. They would not, in another context, choose to do the 'unskilled' tasks they are given, and yet they see it as part of their contribution to the ministry of Lee Abbey, and as their offering, ultimately, to God: *'whatever* you do, whether in word or deed, do it all in the name of the Lord Jesus, giving thanks to God the Father through him' (Col. 3:17). Of course, there is a difference between a deliberate act of corporate worship, and the 'rest of life'. It is all too easy to say glibly, 'all of my life is worship', as an excuse for never meeting together to worship God. But the work of the community is very much part of its commitment and offering to God in the way expressed in Romans 12:1: 'Therefore, I urge you, brothers and sisters, in view of God's mercy, to offer your bodies as living sacrifices, holy and pleasing to God – this is your spiritual act of worship.' As one community member expressed it: 'Worshipping with those I spend my week working with makes the experience more meaningful.'

When a community member is asked to make the weekly holy communion not just the central act of his/her worship, but also the central act of his/her work, it encompasses all that is expressed by communal living – faith, corporate commitment and work. There is no separation between the sacred and the secular, the holy and the practical. Work is worship and worship is work.

The local church is not a focused, intentional community, and whilst people meet on Sundays and at other times for worship, and whilst many churches would aspire to be communities, there is not the same level of shared living and working closely together. Yet sharing in holy communion is still at the centre of the building of community in the local church. Of course, some of what makes a church a community will happen outside corporate worship as believers care for each other and share aspects of their lives. However, the act of breaking bread together is the place where community is formed, as those who gather are fed together on that which sustains the community – the presence of Jesus Christ in the power of the Holy Spirit. In sharing bread and wine we are nourished for the journey and we *become* community: 'Because there is one loaf, we, who are many, are one body, for we all partake of the one loaf' (1 Cor. 10:17). Community is made not by anything we do but by what we share – the story of our redemption in bread broken and wine poured out.

Worshipping together is the primary means by which we express God's will for a unified people. It has the potential to build the body of Christ, to realise Christian family, as well as the power to divide it. Corporate worship is not only an expression of unity. Its quality and depth also sometimes reveals the quality of relationships in the community. Problems in the life of the community are often laid bare in corporate worship. On the other hand, many Christians testify to the way in which good relationships in church enable worship to be more honouring to God and positive for those engaged in it.

So how, in the church community, can we best express the significance of worship for the rest of life and work? How can we make sure that worship is renewing, feeding, equipping and all the things it needs to be for life? And most of all, how do we give God his worth?

Reality

Corporate worship is not always the easiest place to be yourself. At times the subconscious expectation that we will put on our 'Sunday best' extends to more than what we wear. And yet as the body of Christ we are called to know each other's joys and sorrows, to 'rejoice with those who rejoice; mourn with those who mourn' (Rom. 12:15). Whilst it is neither practical nor advisable for every act of worship to reflect the emotions of every person in the congregation, there is certainly the potential for more (or less) connection with the present reality of those who gather to worship. Christopher Cocksworth tells the story of a service he attended during which a woman collapsed at the back of church. Various attempts were made to revive her and eventually an ambulance was called, the paramedics came in and she was taken off to hospital. During all of this commotion the leader continued with the service, without making any reference to what was going on at the back![7] That is an extreme example, but it shows that it is still possible to be more or less 'real', connected and human in worship. Do we put on our Sunday faces, or do we feel at liberty to be 'open to be known for who we are', to quote another of the Lee Abbey promises?

Worship that reflects the realities of the life of the community is refreshing, but also challenging and painful sometimes. In the Lee Abbey communities our close living means we are often very aware of each other's joys and pains. There was a communion service at Lee Abbey Devon where a member of the community had just learned of the death of his father-in-law. Whatever had been planned for that service went out of the window as time was spent comforting and praying for him and his wider family. Many churches will recognise the sensitive paradox of engaging with great joy in the life of one church member (a birth or marriage, for example) whilst also sharing in the pain of another (miscarriage, divorce, illness, bereavement). These events are all the more marked when they occur in the church family simul-taneously. The challenge is to hold together the celebrating and the lamenting, and to find ways of expressing both in authentic worship.

Resonance

Worship is an expression of praise of our God. It is also an expression of the life of the community doing the worshipping. In this way corporate worship needs to embrace the themes of the community. Perhaps this was easier in the past when a shared sense of the rhythm of nature dictated important events; when the whole community was actively engaged in harvest, for example. However, even in today's busy and diverse church communities, there is still a need to make the way in which worship is expressed resonate with the lives of the people gathered.[8]

Community members at Lee Abbey Devon and London take it in turns each morning to lead Morning Prayer. One consequence of this shared leadership is that the reflection on the Bible reading each day comes from that person's perspective as they interpret it for the rest. At its best, this ensures that morning prayers are pertinent to the current life of the community.

Whilst community members might know each other's lives fairly well, the challenge (at least in remote, rural Devon) is to stay in touch with the wider world. This has not always been done well and there have been times when a major global event has gone unnoticed until several days later. However, many community members do feel the imperative to stay in touch with world events. The day the 7/7 bombs went off in London, in Devon guests and community alike needed a point of expression for their shock and bewilderment. A time of prayer was hastily organised in the Chapel and people were able to express their thoughts to each other and to God.

So how might worship reflect the concerns of the everyday life of the community when the community is a church that does not live together? The first step seems to be a need for an awareness on the part of those planning and leading worship of what the lives of people who gather on a Sunday are like from Monday to Saturday. One local church in North Devon has a 'TTT' time in its Sunday service. This is where the vicar interviews someone in the congregation and asks them what they will be doing 'This Time Tomorrow'.[9] It is essential that those preparing any worship event take care to watch the news or read the papers before they do so. Many clergy were 'caught out' by the fact that they had not heard the news of the death of Princess Diana on the night of Saturday, 31 August 1997 and so were not able to engage with the shock of many of their congregation on Sunday morning.

A shared space

It (almost) goes without saying that 'the church' refers to the
body of worshipping people and not the building they worship
in. However, the worship space contributes significantly to the
expression and the meaning of worship. If you were to ask any
guest at Lee Abbey Devon where the hub of the community is,
they are likely to answer, 'the Octagonal Lounge' – a beautiful,
grand, Victorian hall with eight sides, three doorways and four
large, arched windows with panoramic views over the bay and
surrounding hills. It is also the room that is used for most corporate worship. Although there is also a Chapel, a peaceful space
tucked into the eaves of the house, the Octagonal Lounge is the
place that most people associate with the worshipping life of Lee
Abbey. It is a good space to worship in. Why? It has been worshipped in for the 60 years of Lee Abbey's history and the walls
seemed to have soaked all that in. One chaplain used to intro-
duce services by inviting people to relax because 'you're worshipping in our living-room'. It is a big space, and so it also
speaks of the grandeur of God. Its octagonal shape lends itself to
seating people in a circular pattern, reinforcing the images of
community and fellowship. But most of all, it is a room that is
used for other things too. Sometimes it is laid out as a lounge
where people sit and chat and drink tea. Sometimes it is a theatre
where concerts and plays are staged. Sometimes it's a nightclub
where the community dance and party. It is a multi-purpose
room. So when it is used for worship, it expresses the fact that
worshipping God and doing all the other things we do (eating,
chatting, dancing, laughing, singing) are not separate activities,
but are inextricably linked. God is interested in the whole of life
and when several things happen in one room, the holy and the
ordinary become one and God finds his way into every corner of
our lives.

This sense of being 'at home' in a worship space finds
expressions in the other Lee Abbey communities too. Stella
Weaver, the leader of the community Household in Blackburn,

has designated a small walk-in cupboard in her three-bedroomed semi as a 'prayer room' and set up candles and a place to sit and pray. Soon after she moved in, she received a knock on her door and found a little girl standing there who said, 'Excuse me, but I've heard you have a church in your house and if anyone's sick you can come and light a candle and pray. My grandma's sick. Can I?' The ease and accessibility of a cupboard in the house down the road (as opposed to the possible intimidation of a 'proper' church building) is not lost on the people of this deprived outer-urban estate. Likewise, the midweek holy communion that Stella holds in her home, with the help of a local priest, is attracting more and more people who would not usually come to church, but feel at home in her living-room.

The Lee Abbey London community has recently held open evenings to which the student residents are encouraged to come and explore issues of faith. The conscious decision was made to hold these in the more relaxed and informal Garden Room, a place where the residents meet for other purposes too, rather than in the chapel, which might be associated too much with things 'religious' and therefore might be more intimidating.

Many local churches have now caught the vision for encouraging people to see the church building as a place where they can feel at home, and where all the concerns of their lives can find a focus. Some churches have grasped the significance of the use of their buildings for activities for the wider community, with re-orderings of church buildings incorporating areas for the local community to meet, eat and play, as well as worship. It is a true expression of community when the sacred space is also comfortable and available for everyday activity.

A shared process

The work of the people
Liturgy (*leitourgia* in Greek) literally means 'work of the people'. Worship is the work of the people in that all participate and

bring their act of worship together. But worship planning and preparation can also be seen as the work of the people.

Practically speaking, several people's ideas are better than one. Using the gifts and creativity of people of different ages, walks of life and church traditions in the preparation and delivery of corporate worship can richly enhance the act of worship. The benefit of having several people involved in the planning is that it is more likely to represent authentically the concerns and experiences of the community as a whole. There is a rightness about church leaders (and ordained leaders in eucharistic services) playing their proper role in the worship life of a community, but the process of planning and delivering worship as a team is more concordant with Paul's body imagery.

Like everything else that happens at Lee Abbey Devon, the process of planning worship is very much a shared one, done in teams. The weekly holy communion is planned by a team comprising the person preaching that day (who may be one of the chaplains, or someone else), the President (always an ordained minister) and two other community members drawn from a team who feel a calling to be involved in this aspect of community life. Communion services for guests are also planned with input from preacher, president and the team of community members assigned to host the house-party or conference. There are reasons for this team planning that embrace the practical as well as the theological. The fact that worship-planning teams consist of different people each week means that there is always a freshness and a uniqueness about what they plan. The difference is to be found not only in the changing personnel but in the changing relationships between them. It is the interaction between team members that produces the creativity and inspiration.

Those at the forefront of the alternative worship movement write of the significance of planning worship together, of how this process is an end in itself, building community and enabling reflection on the relationship of the community with God. Jonny Baker writes:

The process of discussing ideas, drawing together the raw materials to work from, going away and creatively and prayerfully writing a song or filming a video sequence, finding some music tracks to use, feels somehow charged with the presence of God before we even get to the service.[10]

Sharing in the process of planning worship provides an ideal opportunity for people to discover and develop their gifts, fulfilling the prerogative of the body to help each other to grow up in faith. The accountability and security of a team setting means the responsibility is not all one person's. People can try new things gradually. This is risky, because you don't always know how 'well' people are going to do things, but it's tremendously rewarding when team members discover and use their God-given gifts. Many community members have done things for the first time in worship at Lee Abbey, and some have discovered a call to church leadership in the process. One woman from the Devon community realised that God was calling her to explore vocation to the priesthood when she administered the chalice at communion and found tears streaming down her face.

Working in teams is one of the key skills that community members learn at Lee Abbey, whether it is in a kitchen team making soup or in a worship team making a service. It is a skill that those in the Church will have to learn increasingly. In the Church of England, there is a renewed emphasis on collaborative ministry, lay and ordained, as clergy numbers reduce and the gifts of the laity are rightly encouraged. The process of learning to work well in a team is as important as what the team comes up with. Worship planning is one area in which clergy/lay teams might clearly express collaborative team working, not just out of necessity, 'because there aren't enough clergy to cover all the services' (especially when an incumbent has responsibility for several churches), but because planning teams build community, develop gifts, enable authentic expressions of worship, are theologically consistent with the body of Christ and can be enjoyable!

Inclusiveness

'There is neither Jew nor Greek, slave nor free, male nor female, for you are all one in Christ Jesus' (Gal. 3:28). One of the 'benefits of his passion' is the breaking down of walls of hostility and suspicion between people and groups.

One area where this is particularly seen is in the collaboration between men and women. At Lee Abbey Devon, now both men and women are chaplains and worship leaders, preachers and presidents. It has not always been the case, but gender equality is now a key feature of the ministry. Several people have commented that the issues surrounding the ordination of women that seemed so important in their home churches grow less significant in the context of an open and loving community where people are known and valued for who they are in Christ and given roles according to gifting rather than gender. It is entirely plausible (indeed it has happened) at Lee Abbey Devon that a service might be led by a female president, with a female preacher and music leader, with an all-male dance group performing a worship dance – and for this to happen without special comment! The community has come to accept the normality of men and women working together in whatever role God has given them, so that it has become unremarkable, yet it remains a witness to the wider Church.

There will be other barriers that can, and need to be, broken down in the context of worship (old and young, able bodied and those with special needs, for instance). Barriers of denomination are broken down as people learn to live and worship together. There have been occasions where community members from one church tradition have had to learn to live and worship alongside people from entirely different traditions (strongly Protestant French Baptists with Romanian Roman Catholics, for example). This has often been an enriching experience on both sides as people learn to see relationships with people rather than denominational dogma as the important thing, and to receive from each other's traditions.

A secure place

Community is a place of refuge and safety, where the worshipper is able to feel secure with others in God's presence. The Lee Abbey communities express something of this sense of refuge. A group of local clergy gathers at the household in Blackburn weekly for a time of prayer and breakfast in a way that has been described by one as an 'act of kindness' – a place of retreat and refreshment. Many guests describe Lee Abbey Devon as a 'safe place', away from the pressures and expectations of everyday life, where God is encountered in a new way. Community members, too, testify to their time at Lee Abbey being a time of growth and freedom to explore who they are in a 'safe place', where they are loved and accepted. This sense of security comes in part from the presence of a committed and prayerful community living out God's call. The daily prayer times and weekly holy communion provide frameworks of regular worship that enable and support this sense of safety. As any parent knows, boundaries and structures provide the security a child needs to experiment and embark on new ventures.

Ritual and tradition

Every community, be it a household, or a church, or a neighbourhood, does things that enable it to say, 'We do it like this ...' Such rituals range from 'We always have pasta on Tuesdays', to 'This is the way we celebrate the Eucharist'. However imaginatively worship is expressed, there will always need to be an element of ritual. All churches have rituals. Even those that would consider themselves to be the most 'free' and spontaneous have phrases, signals and rituals that are recognisable by the community. Rituals provide a sense of place, belonging and 'home'. They provide boundaries, a framework for belonging and a sense of continuity with what has gone before. They build community.

Order in worship was very important to Paul, 'for God is not a God of disorder but of peace' (1 Cor. 14:33). And so he encourages order and propriety in worship: 'When you come together, everyone has a hymn, or a word of instruction, a revelation, a tongue or interpretation. All of these must be done for the strengthening of the Church ... But everything should be done in a fitting and orderly way' (1 Cor. 14:26–40).

The rituals and traditions of the worshipping community provide the security from which to branch out into creativity and risk. You can't have 'new' until you have 'old', nor 'innovative' until you have 'standard', nor 'creative' until you have 'commonplace'. It is from the secure base of received traditions and structures that we branch out to discover new ways of doing things, and in the process we rediscover and enliven the traditions. Even those involved at the cutting edge of experimental worship recognise the essential presence of long-held traditions and rituals: 'In post-modern times, when so little is fixed and everything is in flux, tradition and continuity actually offer a sense of the weight of history, an anchor point.'[11] The key task facing the Church in worship is to find ways of enabling the interaction of set structures, traditions and expectations with playful (even mischievous) experimentation – what N. T. Wright calls 'faithful improvisation'.[12] As Christians we have a rich and exciting tradition to play with. One of the most stimulating things happening in worship is the re-imagining and re-presenting of valued traditions for today's culture.

Experimenting

Some churches, often inspired by the alternative worship scene, have begun to experiment with new ways of expressing ancient traditions. Lee Abbey Devon has found the tradition of labyrinths and prayer stations to be an important source of worship and prayer for many guests who come seeking space and time to explore their faith. Inspired by Tim Lomax's work on Liquid worship,[13] one evening holy communion was laid out in the different rooms around the house in zones (preparation, confession, the word, the sermon, intercession) at which people could spend as much time as they liked and which they could visit in any order. At each were interactive activities for people to engage in (nailing written sins to a large wooden cross, for example). One woman fed back afterwards that she had been nervous about the idea beforehand, but the fact that 'traditional' liturgy from *Common Worship* was used (the Prayer of Humble Access was hung from a ceiling in sections and one had to walk through it as one prayed it) had put her at ease, she said. It was familiar, yet different.

A risky place

Community can be a safe place, but it is rightly a risky place too. Anyone who takes seriously the challenge of building and living in community exposes themselves to the risk of knowing and being known deeply, discovering the worst side of themselves and others as well as the best. Community is nothing if it is not a community of real people, 'warts and all', together realising that they cannot ever be everything to each other. As Henri Nouwen writes:

> The support of the Christian community is a support in common expectation. That requires constant criticism of anyone who makes the community a safe shelter or a cosy clique, and a constant encouragement to look forward to what is to come.[14]

The same is true of our worship. Although we build community in and through our worship and are built by it, it will never be perfect. The laudable motivation of making our worship the best it can be can lead to the need to have it all sorted, pinned down and pigeon-holed. There is always a temptation to make worship in our own image. We may forget that we worship an almighty and unpredictable God. We may forget that anything could happen, despite (or maybe occasionally *because of*) our most careful planning.

We worship a God who is good, but is neither tame nor safe,

and as such our worship may be neither and may lead to
something altogether more hazardous and breath-taking than we
had intended. Worship is always to be risky, challenging and
exciting if it is to reflect the nature of the God to whom it is
directed, and we must be prepared to stand on the edge. As the
writer to the Hebrews says, our worship is to be reverent,
always, but also full of awe and wonder, 'for our God is a con-
suming fire' (Heb. 12:28). Mike Riddell expresses vividly the
excitement of the kind of worship which is faithful to the ancient
traditions and yet risks stepping out into new places:

> Some ... have sought to recapture worship as something
> which leaps wet and wild from the bog of captivated
> hearts; which stretches convention until it rips and allows
> God in; which draws words and symbols from the raw
> experience of participants and flings them to God in love
> and desperation.[15]

The risk of creativity

This climate of exploration and freedom is reflected in the worship at Lee Abbey Devon. Although Anglican in framework, the
community is outside diocesan structures and is classed as a
place at liberty to explore experimental forms of worship. Some
factors remain constant. For example, an authorised communion
prayer is always used (from an Anglican or another tradition) at
holy communion. But even this can be creatively expressed. We
have experimented with the eucharistic prayer being mimed at
the same time it is read, and often with images and words pro-
jected onto a screen. A communion service will invariably have
the essential elements of confession and absolution, but these
may be done in different ways – for example, burning written
'sins' in a fireplace. At many services at Lee Abbey the creative
arts – drama, dance and music – are an integral part, and in each
of these new and creative ways are found of expressing the
truths of the Gospel. An important underlying principle is that

different people receive and process information in different ways. Some people love to hear sermons and respond in words. Others prefer the visual and the experiential. Drama and music may 'connect' with their spirituality. At the Youth Camp one year, as the sermon was given by the preacher, it was interpreted by an artistic team member in art, resulting in some spectacular and moving pieces. Another benefit of creativity in worship is the chance it offers to involve more people with different gifts and skills. In this sense it builds community.

Of course, where there is creativity there is always the risk of worship becoming more concerned with itself than with God, of entertainment rather than engagement being paramount, and of the worshipper being seen as the consumer. Ian Stackhouse warns against 'the pressure to make something happen. Worship as spiritual formation is sidelined in favour of worship as effect.'[16]

I have already said that one of the great joys of the Lee Abbey communities is their denominational diversity. However, along with that comes the danger that those leading worship feel that they have to 'provide something to suit everyone'. This is the experience of many church leaders with diverse congregations. The perceived need to 'keep everyone happy' can lead to a frantic consumerism in which the true goal and aim of worship is forgotten. Eddie Gibbs and Ian Coffey comment:

> Worship must not be used for other means that result in its becoming subverted and diverted. Worship is not entertainment. It is not an expression of cultural elitism. It is not religious education. It is not emotional self-indulgence or a vehicle for evangelism. Worship does not produce a quick fix but flows out into the whole of life, and the whole of life is drawn into worship.[17]

The risk of being changed

One of the challenges facing any Christian community, be it a church or an intentional community, is developing good and authentic patterns of worship, enabling both freedom and ritual to have their place, encouraging and respecting diversity in worship style and format whilst retaining core distinctives.

In worship one risks being changed, and that is not always a comfortable process. As we worship alongside others who come from different traditions, we are challenged by differences in worship style and doctrinal emphasis to see beyond what we had thought was important and to see another's point of view. We are challenged to make sacrifices in 'what I like' in favour of what helps others, in the spirit of Philippians 2: 'Do nothing out of selfish ambition or vain conceit, but in humility consider others better than yourselves. Each of you should look not only to your own interests, but also to the interests of others.' We are challenged by the exciting and sometimes testing process of planning and worshipping alongside others. Most of all, we allow ourselves to be changed by the God whom, as a community, we worship 'in spirit and in truth'.

NOTES
1. See, e.g., Deut. 6:13; Luke 4:8.
2. See, e.g., 1 Cor. 14:3; 12:7.
3. Henri Nouwen, *Reaching Out* (Fount, 1998), p. 123.
4. Dietrich Bonhoeffer, *Life Together* (SCM, 1954), p. 96.
5. *Common Worship*, Eucharistic Prayer H.
6. There have also been members of the Devon community who come from Roman Catholic backgrounds. Some have felt able to take bread and wine at Corpus, others have not. Some have also had the provision of receiving the sacraments at the local Roman Catholic church in Lynton.
7. Christopher Cocksworth & Rosalind Brown, *Being a Priest Today* (Canterbury Press, 2002), p. 73.
8. David Runcorn makes a helpful distinction between 'relevance' and 'resonance' in his *Spirituality Workbook* (SPCK, 2006), p. 70.

9. Mark Greene's book *Thank God it's Monday* (Scripture Union, 1997) helps those leading corporate worship to understand the themes of the working lives of congregation members. The London Institute for Contemporary Christianity produces helpful resource materials on faith and the workplace.

10. Jonny Baker, 'Rhythm of the Masses' in *Mass Culture: Eucharist and mission in a post-modern world* (BRF, 1999), p. 48.

11. Jonny Baker, 'Ritual as Strategic Practice' in *The Rite Stuff*, ed. Pete Ward (BRF, 2004), p. 93.

12. N. T. Wright, *The New Testament and the People of God* (London, SPCK, 1992), pp. 140–43.

13. See, for example, Tim Lomax & Michael Moynagh, *Liquid Worship* (Grove Books W181).

14. Henri Nouwen, *Reaching Out* (Fount, 1998), p. 120.

15. Mike Riddell, *Threshold of the Future* (SPCK, 1998), p. 143.

16. Ian Stackhouse, *The Gospel-Driven Church* (Paternoster, 2004), p. 48.

17. Eddie Gibbs & Ian Coffey, *Church Next* (IVP, 2001), p. 152.

5

John and Gay Perry

COMMUNITY AND HEALING

Rt Revd John Perry and Mrs Gay Perry were members, and he was Warden, of the Devon Community from 1977 to 1989. John has since been Bishop of Southampton and Bishop of Chelmsford. Gay has a particular interest in the rehabilitation of sufferers from drug and alcohol addiction. John chaired the Burrswood Trustees and the House of Bishops Working Party Report A Time to Heal. *He currently chairs the Council of the Lee Abbey movement.*

The Lee Abbey communities have often been referred to as centres of renewal and healing – safe places where God's presence and restorative power is experienced. In obedience to the example and command of Jesus Christ, the early pioneers of Lee Abbey, Devon – Roger de Pemberton, Geoffrey Rogers, Leslie Sutton and Jack Winslow – ensured that the ministry of healing was a natural, integral part of the community's life and of its ministry to the guests. Teaching, preaching and healing were, and continue to be, all of one piece in sharing the good news.

This made a strong impact on us during one of our earlier visits to Lee Abbey, Devon. It was back in the early 1960s, when John had been appointed as the first vicar of St Andrew's, Chorleywood, a new parish in Hertfordshire. The principles of community living, expressing the corporate life of the church as the body of Christ, were ones that we longed to see developed in our own parish. Words were not enough. Authentication was needed in the commitment of church members to care for one another and the local community.

Over the years that followed, the ministry of healing, encouraged by members of the medical and other caring professions, was gradually developed. It was a bumpy and costly journey. Hard questions had to be faced about the mystery of suffering and healing. 'Why are some healed and others not?' Perseverance in prayer and sometimes fasting was required. We realised our complete dependence upon God's power, and the truth of Jesus' words, 'apart from me you can do nothing' (John 15:5).

Along the way, we also learnt a great deal from the community life of the early Church, as we read and studied the Acts of the Apostles. J. B. Phillips wrote:

> No one can read this book without being convinced that there is Someone here at work besides mere human beings. Perhaps because of their very simplicity, perhaps because of their readiness to believe, to obey, to give, to suffer, and if need be to die, the Spirit of God found what surely He must always be seeking – a fellowship of men and women so united in love and faith that He can work in them and through them with the minimum of let or hindrance.[1]

That vibrancy of faith and openness to be a channel of the healing power of God is illustrated in a delightfully humorous story about Leslie Sutton, recounted by Jack Winslow:[2]

> Before joining the community, Leslie served as a missionary in the Congo where shortly after arriving he fell ill.

As he lay in bed with a very high temperature Juji, a young Christian, came in from school. 'May I read to you, bwana?' he asked. Leslie thought he wanted to show off his reading. 'Yes, do read to me, Juji,' he said. Juji read the story of the raising of Lazarus, and then asked, 'Bwana, if Jesus could do that for Lazarus, couldn't He heal you?' 'Yes,' said Leslie, 'will you ask Him?' Juji knelt by the bed with hands folded in prayer. 'Father God, you've brought this white man here to teach us, and now he's fallen ill. Please, Father God, make him well, and make him well now.' Then he got up, threw off the bedclothes and said, 'Now, you can get up, bwana, and I'll make you a cup of tea.' Leslie reached out for his thermometer. He was completely normal.

Jack Winslow then asks, 'Is not our chief need to ask of God the faith of a child?'

In the unfolding story of those early years of the founding and growth of Lee Abbey in Devon, the unshakeable faith of Leslie, Jack, Geoffrey and Roger in the transforming power of God, helped to focus the life of the community on a God with whom nothing is impossible.

A theology of healing

The closest Old Testament word for 'health' is *shalom*. One of the covenant names for God was *Yahweh-shalom*. The root meaning of *shalom* is totality and wholeness, and can also be translated as soundness in life and limb, and wholeness of heart. *Shalom* denotes the presence of wholeness, completeness and well-being in all spheres of life – physical, mental and spiritual – and encompasses personal, social, national and global relationships. *Shalom* relates to the individual's need for health, and the need of a healthy community and healthy environment. *Shalom* embraces the whole of creation and its longing for liberation and healing.

Peace and healing are frequently set alongside each other (Isa. 57:19; Jer. 14:19), and *shalom* is the need of a wounded people

(Jer. 6:14). At the heart of it all, *shalom* is about living in a right relationship with God and with others, out of which the 'good life' can be fully experienced. It comes as the climax of the Aaronic blessing: 'The Lord turn his face to you and give you peace [*shalom*]' (Num. 6:26).

In the New Testament healing is rooted in the ministry of Jesus, who 'went about doing good and healing all manner of diseases among the people'. The manifesto for his mission and ministry was made clear when he read from the scroll of the prophet Isaiah in the synagogue in his home town of Nazareth:

> 'The Spirit of the Lord is upon me because he has anointed me to bring good news to the poor. He has sent me to proclaim release to the captives and recovery of sight to the blind, to let the oppressed go free, to proclaim the year of the Lord's favour.' Then Jesus declared: 'Today this Scripture has been fulfilled in your hearing' (Luke 4:18–21).

The gauntlet was thrown down. Proclamation and healing were to be combined throughout his ministry.

The most explicit mention of this combination occurs first in Matthew 4:23: 'Jesus went throughout Galilee, teaching in their synagogues and proclaiming the good news of the kingdom and curing every disease and every sickness among the people.' In turn, this was the pattern that Jesus set for the mission of the 12 disciples (Luke 9) and the 72 other followers (Luke 10), sending them out to preach the Kingdom of God and to heal the sick. In the Acts of the Apostles and the Epistles the ministry of healing was integral to the life and witness of the early Christian communities. Praying 'in the name of Jesus' underlined the authority and power which they had been given (e.g. Acts 3:1–10).

The Letter of James offers a model for the ministry of healing in the local church (5:14–16). The leaders (elders) take responsibility to pray, almost certainly with the laying on of hands, after the example of Jesus himself, and anointing with oil, which is associated with healing in the Bible. Expectant faith is exercised.

Furthermore, the importance of forgiveness, given and received, not only for the sick person but also amongst other church members, is stressed as essential in the process of healing. James conveys a powerful picture of a church community praying, caring and supporting one another and discovering the healing love of God that includes everyone, not just the person(s) who is visibly ill. Indeed, a church that is strong on teaching and preaching but is not committed to a ministry of healing is selling people short. Bishop Morris Maddocks affirms:

> Christian healing is, first and foremost, about Christ. It follows the pattern He set in His own ministry, and the commission He gave to His disciples, and the fact that it happens at all is the fruit of His work, both in the creation, and in the salvation of mankind. In both these mighty works, humankind has been created and recreated in the image of God – has been made whole. This is what distinguishes Christian healing from other types of healing. It is the whole work of Christ, in a person's body, mind and spirit, designed to bring that person to that wholeness which is God's will for us all.[3]

This holistic understanding of healing is also emphasised in a major report, *A Time to Heal*:

> The Christian Ministry of Healing is: Visionary – because it beckons us towards the future and a glimpse of the Kingdom: creation renewed in perfect health and wholeness. Prophetic – because it calls us to reconsider our relationships with God, each other and the world, and to seek forgiveness and a new start in our lives. Dynamic – because Jesus Christ is with us till the end of time: when we pray for his help, he comforts, strengthens and heals us, responding to our deepest needs.

Wounded healers

Over the years, the theology of healing has had to be lived and worked out in the experience and ministry of the various communities that are part of the Lee Abbey movement. While we were in the Lee Abbey community in Devon, guests would frequently say, 'How marvellous it must be to live in community.' In one sense they were right; but life together in community is a constantly changing process in which relationships, attitudes and priorities have to be worked at and reviewed. If there is to be growth in depth, there has to be a willingness to go the way of the cross with one another: guarding against exclusiveness; shutting our hearts to no one; being sensitive towards one another and not causing unnecessary hurt; facing and dealing with conflict; supporting one another in weakness and weariness; affirming one another gladly; responding in obedience to the Holy Spirit's penetrating and sometimes painful work of corporate renewal and healing. Unless this is allowed to happen within the community itself, the ministry of healing offered to guests can be hollow and ineffective.

Following the breakdown of a relationship, a former community member wrote: 'I'm learning that what matters in this life is not *what* happens to you but what you do with it in the Lord. If each disaster, pain, suffering, failure, is allowed to be ploughed earth for the seeds of grace, then love, humility, faith and obedience can only grow the more for it all.'

Inevitably, there are always guests who reflect current problems and set-backs – marital breakdown, family dysfunction, unemployment and redundancy, alcoholism and drug abuse, rejection and loneliness. Behind the brave 'front' there are often deep hurts and tensions that only the love of Jesus can ultimately heal. Through the caring and sensitivity of the community, his accepting, healing love can be mediated.

Frequently, clergy and other lay leaders arrive feeling that they have reached the end of their resources and know their need for fresh vision and courage. Counsel and prayer before returning home can enable them to face the responsibilities of leadership that have been entrusted to them. In turn, as wounded healers they are able to bring to the churches they serve a fresh perspective on what it means to belong to the body of Christ.

We well remember a clergy couple who came to us after only 18 months in a parish and ready to give up. Battered and discouraged by criticism, they had even lost their desire for God. They had no hope in their hearts that the situation could change, but by the end of the week, after rest and refreshment, they began to hear God's voice again. He spoke to them through his word: 'May the God of hope fill you with all joy and peace as you trust in him, so that you may overflow with hope by the power of the Holy Spirit' (Rom. 15:13). They went away with a new song in their hearts and stayed on in the parish. The next time we saw them was when they returned with a group from their parish. Healing indeed!

Lee Abbey Households are at the cutting edge of this kind of vulnerability. Members of these Households have chosen to 'be where Jesus is' amongst the poor and disadvantaged, the powerless and isolated, yet also sharing in the richness of racial, cultural and religious diversity. Martin and Suzette Young, who were leaders of the community Household in Aston, Birmingham, for ten years, reflected:

> When we touch illness, hardship, sinfulness, suffering of any kind, we choose to suffer alongside – sharing the suffering of Jesus. We don't carry the sin of others, only Jesus can do that and has done that, but we touch the pain of the results of the sin as it affects us and the families around us. The numerous shooting incidents around the streets of Aston have become almost, sadly, commonplace. We do not know what long-term effect it has on one, but spiritually it feels like bearing the pain of the city in our prayers and weeping over it as Jesus did.

The Households in Birmingham, Blackburn and Bristol are all seen as oases of welcome and friendship, listening and acceptance, safety and support. Those who come to visit or stay find renewed strength and the healing presence of Jesus – a far cry from the general stress of inner-city living. In their ministry of hospitality, community members often find that their role is simply 'holding people steady', whether that be in fragile relationships, single parenthood, debt crisis, chronic illness, racial intimidation, robbery and mugging. Shirina, a young Asian woman from a Muslim background, wrote:

> I came to Lee Abbey Aston in a state of no hope, and felt condemned by every Christian I knew. I was so depressed and felt so much pain that death seemed to be the only way out. At the Aston community I was loved, accepted for who I was, and I was listened to. They taught me to see me as God sees me, and that I am no longer a victim but a survivor, and that I matter to God. God brought healing to me through his love and through the unconditional love that I received. My time at Lee Abbey Aston saved my life, and helped me to move on in God and in life.

Writing out of many years of experience in the L'arche communities, Henri Nouwen's hope-filled realism touches a chord:

> Nothing is sweet or easy about community. Community is a fellowship of people who do not hide their joys and sorrows but make them visible to each other in a gesture of hope. In community we say, 'Life is full of gains and losses, joys and sorrows, ups and downs – but we do not have to live it alone. We want to drink our cup together and thus celebrate the truth that the wounds of our individual lives, which seem intolerable when lived alone, become sources of healing when we live them as part of a fellowship of mutual care.'[4]

Healing and evangelism

The founders of Lee Abbey had a strong commitment to evangelism – to see people discovering the liberating power of the good news of Jesus Christ. The years that have followed have witnessed this same commitment to an evangelistic ministry, albeit expressed in different ways in the different parts of the movement. The approach to evangelism is not the same in the Lee Abbey International Students' Club in Earls Court, London, or in the Households in Birmingham, Blackburn and Bristol, as in Lee Abbey, Devon. But all the communities share the same conviction that their community life needs to be a visible and tangible expression of the reconciling, healing power of Jesus Christ – a healing that is first and foremost a spiritual one, bringing freedom from the grip of sin, and peace with God through the saving, healing power of the cross of Jesus (1 Pet. 2:24–25).

When four friends brought a paralysed man to Jesus, he immediately discerned that the paralytic's primary need was one of forgiveness. 'Friend, your sins are forgiven,' Jesus declared. Then he said, 'I tell you, get up, take your mat and go home.' The man immediately 'stood up before them, took what he had been lying on and went to his home, glorifying God' (Luke 5:18–26). Jesus' approach to healing was a fully integrated, holistic one. Furthermore, his healing led to discipleship.

Often in the New Testament healing and evangelism go together – the one flowing naturally from the other. When a healing takes place the ripples can go far beyond the one concerned. Others who may be sceptical and questioning are confronted with undeniable evidence of the presence and power of God who heals today. Whether this takes place in a community like Lee Abbey or in a local church where the ministry of healing is firmly rooted, the Holy Spirit is constantly at work, drawing people to discover for themselves the friendship and redeeming love of Christ.

We vividly recall the first occasion when a large group from several deaneries in the Cotswolds, under the leadership of their Rural Dean, Canon Arthur Dodds, came to stay at Lee Abbey, Devon. Their initial apprehension was quickly dispelled. In the days that followed many experienced the healing touch of God in different ways, not least in relationships. Significantly, the life of the community made its own unobtrusive impact. Moreover, the service of prayer with the laying on of hands – a regular feature in the weekly programme – was a particular blessing to many. Out of this, and subsequent visits, as well as a community team mission in the Cotswolds, the spiritual life in that area gained fresh vision and impetus.

A significant outcome of this partnership was the founding of the Harnhill Centre of Christian Healing near Cirencester. Harnhill Manor became the home of a small community, backed up by a large number of non-residential helpers. In the years that have followed it has gone from strength to strength, and is a beacon of light to encourage many from far and wide to receive counsel, prayer and teaching. The burgeoning growth of centres for healing like Harnhill is indicative of the deep spiritual, emotional, as well as physical needs of many hurting people today. It was Bishop John V. Taylor who said:

> He or she is whole who is joined to the suffering of others. To be made whole, to be saved, is not only to be set free from sin, it is also to be joined to sin, to be joined with Christ to the whole sin-sick world. And that is a far greater suffering than any from which we may have been relieved. We can bear it only in the blessed, burdened company of all faithful people.[5]

The mystery of healing and suffering

Another centre closely linked to Lee Abbey is Burrswood, near Tunbridge Wells. It is a Christian centre for medical and spiritual care. It includes a small hospital and the Church of Christ the Healer. The community at Burrswood is committed to bringing together medicine and the Christian faith, and to working within the mystery of healing and suffering. It aims to keep the love of Christ at the heart of care and to be a sign of the Kingdom of God in a hurting world.

Burrswood is a fine example of how Christ's concern for the care and the healing of the whole person – body, mind, emotions and spirit – is expressed through a multi-disciplinary approach to healing. It is also a place where the community has to face some of the sharp and searching questions about the mystery of healing and suffering.

A beautiful example of this is Katharine, who was a patient at Burrswood. She had motor-neurone disease and her one remaining movement was blinking. The staff around her had to carry a sheet of Morse code in their pockets because this was her only means of communication – long and short blinks! Dr Gareth Tuckwell, who was the Medical Director, recalls:

> We thought that her care would present a great challenge to the team, that she would have tremendous fears and emotional needs, and yet we encountered someone who was totally at peace. Her eyes radiated the love and presence of Christ and we were all enlarged through knowing her. We received so much from her, and realised that on encountering Katharine, healing had to be re-defined. We had not met anyone so at peace with herself, her illness and, above all, with God.[6]

Michael Mitton, in his book on healing with the intriguing title *Wild Beasts and Angels*,[7] includes a chapter on 'The Mystery of Healing'. Here he writes:

> The trouble with mystery is that there are no obvious answers. We can feel trapped by mystery, a sense of helplessness, which feels frustrated by lack of knowledge, insight and wisdom. That there is a longing that there must be a solution, a final chapter in which some clever detective

puts the clues together and tells us what it all means. The
worst of it is that, when we are suffering and hurting, the
last thing we want to be doing is to be wrestling with life's
greatest mysteries. We want nice clear answers, not awkward puzzles. People often ask 'Why?' in the face of tra-
gedy, and often close behind that 'Why?' is a deep sense of
anger that no one has given a good and simple answer.

And then he goes on to ask that same question in relation to two
close friends. One of them, a Franciscan Brother named Ramon,
dies, and the other, Tony, is cured. The refreshing honesty with
which he struggles with this dilemma strikes a chord for many
people when he adds:

> Whilst clever people can come up with complex attempts to
> explain why a good and powerful God cures some people
> and not others, the rest of us find ourselves nervously
> biting our fingernails, trusting with childlike faith yet
> inwardly uncertain which way the divine vote will go.

Thankfully, Michael Mitton does not leave it there but takes us to
two profound chapters in St Paul's Letter to the Romans. In
chapter 7 the apostle is unashamedly honest about his wrestling
with the potential pitfalls of his own humanity, and then in
chapter 8 he reminds his readers that we are not on our own, that
through and with Christ we are children of God: 'It is that very
Spirit bearing witness with our spirit that we are children of
God, and if children, then heirs of God and joint heirs with
Christ – if, in fact, we are suffering with Him so that we may also
be glorified with Him' (verse 16).

St Paul then invites his readers to bring into the picture the
eternal dimension; that the only way to begin to make sense of
the suffering of this broken world, and the suffering that we
encounter, is to have one eye on the world that is to come: 'I
consider that the sufferings of this present time are not worth
comparing with the glory about to be revealed to us' (verse 18). It

is a majestic chapter climaxing on a note of triumph: 'Who can separate us from the love of Christ?' (verse 35). No one and nothing can take from us the most essential thing – the fact that we are loved by God. Thus Paul answers his own question with joyful confidence: 'nothing will be able to separate us from the love of God in Christ Jesus our Lord' (verse 39).

It is this unshakable conviction and confidence that has to undergird our understanding of and involvement in the mystery of healing, and we must be able to face its tough and searching questions with integrity, hope and trust.

Treasures in the darkness

Sister Ann Machtilde scs said on one occasion: 'We have to enter the dark night ourselves in order to be authentic bearers of the light, and be wounded ourselves in order to bring healing and wholeness to others.' Little did we realise that we would experience something more of the truth of those words when, shortly after we had been asked to write this chapter, Gay was diagnosed with aggressive ovarian cancer with secondaries. As she is normally a very healthy person, this came like a bolt out of the blue. In the months that have followed, amidst the emotional ups and downs, we have discovered fresh experiences of God's encompassing, rock-like love and healing power. The prayers and practical support of many others, sometimes from un-expected sources, have often proved to be 'treasures in the darkness'. We have also found an even greater empathy with those who travel the path of suffering.

When we respond to the suffering of others, we are helping to make tangible God's compassionate presence in our world. Compassion epitomised Jesus' ministry on countless occasions (e.g. Mark 1:40–42; Matt. 20:29–34). Compassion brings healing by creating a community of concern that helps to ensure that those in need are not alone in their pain and fears, but are upheld and strengthened by others who come alongside and journey with them. The Church in each local community should be expressing the compassionate love of Christ, made visible in the care of members for one another and for the wider community. Where compassion is present, the heart of God is revealed, and in the process of healing, treasures of God's grace are found in the darkness.

A parable from nature illustrates this. In December 1981, a hurricane of considerable ferocity hit the North Devon coast and within the brief compass of a couple of hours many acres of trees on the Lee Abbey estate were brought crashing down. The scene afterwards was like a First World War battlefield. Seasoned oaks, which had stood proudly for well over a hundred years, had been uprooted and smashed. The labour of careful conservation over many years was seemingly destroyed. Most of us on the community could not see beyond the devastation. But one much-loved senior member, Ursula Kay, a gifted and inspiring naturalist, brought another perspective. 'Watch out for the re-creative, renewing power of nature', she urged. As time went on, Ursula was proved to be right. Out of the darkness of the hurricane, new treasures were unearthed.

In his book *Fear no Evil*,[8] in which he describes his own encounter with cancer, David Watson reflects:

> There is little doubt that millions of Christians all down the centuries have become more Christ-like through suffering. I know of many who have an almost ethereal beauty about them, refined through pain. In fact, those who have experienced more of the love of God than I have ever met have also endured more suffering. When you crush lavender, you find its full fragrance; when you squeeze an orange, you extract its sweet juice. In the same way it is often through pain and hurts that we develop the fragrance and sweetness of Jesus in our lives.

Healing of the nations

The last book of the Bible, Revelation, describes the vision given
to the aged apostle John of a great river flowing from the throne
of God, bringing life in its wake. On each side of the river stands
the Tree of Life; its leaves are for the 'healing of the nations'
(22:1–6). It is a powerful picture, blending in with another picture of another tree – the cross of Jesus Christ. The tree of shame
that has become the tree of glory; life outpoured in order to bring
life to the world. Down the centuries people from all nations
have found new life, hope and healing at the cross.

From its beginnings, Lee Abbey has always had a strong
international dimension in the composition of its communities,
the guests and the student residents. In the early post-Second
World War years in Devon, guests from Germany and Holland
found reconciliation and healing during their visits. Later, in the
mid 1960s, the Lee Abbey International Students' Club in London was founded, under the leadership of Gordon and Sheila
Mayo. It continues to be a thriving 'home from home' for some
150 students from over 40 nations, cared for in the name of Christ
by an international community.

Not surprisingly, tensions can occasionally arise in the community because of differences of background and culture. David
Bainbridge, the present Warden, who with his wife Mary served
as mission partners with the Church Mission Society in Pakistan,
describes an occasion when a young 'coloured' South African
joined the community:

> He came with a deep sense of past hurts and racial abuse in
> South Africa. He was put on the maintenance team where
> he worked well, but felt very grieved when an opening on
> the Office Team arose and a white South African girl
> bypassed him for the post. He saw this as direct racial
> discrimination, although her spoken English was much
> easier to understand. There was a succession of relatively
> small issues when he accused Lee Abbey of racial

discrimination against him. On each occasion we talked, listened, made whatever concessions seemed reasonable and prayed with him and for him, and he calmed down. We tried hard to give him other jobs, including cleaning the Lee Abbey vehicles, which is one of the maintenance team's responsibilities, but this he took as a serious insult because in South Africa only the 'servants' are asked to clean another man's car. Eventually he got so angry that he stood up at breakfast publicly in front of the resident students, and accused Lee Abbey of racism, and said he was going to lodge an official complaint through the South African Embassy. Within a day of this he took the next flight home.

Two years passed and then David received an email: 'I hope you are all doing well, and I pray that God will richly bless you. Anyway, I'm doing well, but the main reason why I am sending this email is to apologise for the pain that I caused you when I left Lee Abbey, I ask you please to forgive me.' Other emails followed, sharing how he had completed further studies and was now involved with youth work at his local church. Praise God for healing!

Healing and death

Four members of the community died at different points during our time in Devon. Their deaths left a deep mark on us all, and forced us to face up to the reality and inevitability of death. There was no room for triumphalism, yet the pain of acute loss was accompanied by the gentle assurance that death is not the end but the entrance into a fuller life beyond with Christ.

A Christian view of death is rooted in the resurrection of Jesus from the dead. In the New Testament death is viewed almost exclusively through the window of Christ's resurrection. It is no longer the 'last word', a step into oblivion. God's gift of eternal life freely offered to all whose trust is placed in his beloved Son, Jesus Christ, is not terminated by death but is timeless. Jesus himself made the promise: 'I am the resurrection and the life. The one who believes in me will live, even though they die' (John 11:25).

It has been said that in the Christian healing ministry we live on a knife-edge. Death is the opposite of life; illness, if unchecked, can easily lead to death, or at least to impaired life. So death, like illness, is to be fought and life is to be extended where possible. Yet from another perspective death is the greatest healing. Healing or whole-making is a wonderfully eternal thing; always healing is towards eternity. Sometimes God gives his healing gift in death.

In his *Letter of Consolation*[9] Henri Nouwen writes of the importance of befriending our death, of facing up to its significance before we are in any real danger of dying, so that we put death into proper perspective. He asks the question:

> And isn't death, the frightening unknown that lurks in the depths of our unconscious minds, like a great shadow that we perceive only dimly in our dreams? Befriending death seems to be the basis of all other forms of befriending. I have a deep sense, hard to articulate, that if we could really befriend death, we would be free people. So many of our doubts and hesitations, ambivalences and insecurities, are bound up with our deep-seated fear of death, that our lives would be significantly different if we could relate to death as a familiar guest instead of a threatening stranger.

Paul the apostle had clearly seen death in its proper light:

> So we do not lose heart. Even though our outer nature is wasting away, our inner nature is being renewed day by day. For this slight momentary affliction is preparing us for an eternal weight of glory beyond all measure, because we look not on what can be seen, but at what cannot be seen; for that which is seen is temporary, but what cannot be seen is eternal (2 Cor. 4:16–18).

Community life at its best, whether it is a Lee Abbey community or a local church, can be a foretaste of heaven. Whether in joy or in sorrow, belonging to one another in mutual trust and loving support is strengthened by the assurance that the destination is certain. The Lord who is our Shepherd travels with us and goes before us (Psalm 23). We are never alone, and we are part of an eternal community.

Canon John Poulton was not only a wise and visionary Chairman of the Lee Abbey Council back in the 1980s but was also a gifted speaker and writer. On one occasion he was the guest speaker at Lee Abbey, Devon, and in a moving final address prior to an evening holy communion, when there would be prayer with the laying on of hands, he gave an invitation:

> This Maker, this Creator, this Lord invites you to come. Come just as you are to experience His living presence, maybe fully for the first time. Come, opening doors that you have kept bolted until now. Maybe that great big door of self-pity – open it, take it down. Come with your unanswered prayers and your new resolves and your burdens and your illness and your condition, to offer dark and light alike to Him who comes to meet you, to transform you.

The challenge ahead

Communities of faith, hope and love are needed to honeycomb our land and beyond; communities where there is a vibrant expectancy that God can and does heal today. The power to heal belongs to him, not to us. Yet God trusts us to be channels of his healing grace, conduits of the healing streams of the Holy Spirit. In the name of Jesus, there are wounds to be healed; relationships to be repaired; burdens to be shared; fears to be quelled; hopes to be fulfilled. Nothing is impossible with God.

NOTES

1. J. B. Phillips, *The Young Church in Action* (Bles, 1955).

2. Jack Winslow, *Modern Miracles* (Hodder & Stoughton, 1968).

3. Morris Maddocks, *Twenty Questions About Healing* (SPCK, 1981).

4. Henri Nouwen, *Can You Drink the Cup?* (Notre Dame, Indiana, Ave Maria Press, 1996).

5. John V. Taylor, *Change of Address* (Hodder & Stoughton, 1968).

6. Gareth Tuckwell & David Flagg, *A Question of Healing* (Fount, 1995).

7. Michael Mitton, *Wild Beasts and Angels* (DLT, 2000).

8. David Watson, *Fear No Evil* (Hodder & Stoughton, 1984).

9. Henri Nouwen, *A Letter of Consolation* (Harper & Collins, Inc., 1982).

6

David Bainbridge

COMMUNITY AND DIVERSITY

Revd David Bainbridge has been a regular guest at Lee Abbey Devon since 1962. He has taught in Uganda, then with CMS and Scripture Union in Pakistan, followed by 15 years of parish ministry in Bristol. Since 2001 he has been the Warden of the Lee Abbey International Students' Club in London.

The one irreducible truth about humanity is diversity.

Martin Firrell[1]

As the aircraft door opened and we descended onto the tarmac, it felt as though we were entering an oven. We expected and felt prepared for a culture shock, but we were overpowered by the heat, humidity, noise, crowds, dust and smells. Sleep that night was disturbed by the clamour of midnight rickshaws from the cinema next door – then the dawn call to prayer from countless mosques. It was a vivid and unforgettable experience as Mary and I, with our five-month-old first child, began what turned out to be nine years in Lahore, Pakistan in 1975. We started the slow process of adapting to so much that was different and at times scary, yet we longed for comfort in the familiar. Anything, in fact, that reminded us of home in Britain – people, language, food, shops, newspapers, TV ...

Learning how to relate to people who are different from ourselves is crucial today, involving a number of important personal, social and political issues. On the international scene there are questions of immigration and asylum, international terrorism versus the 'war on terror', the rising profile of Asian economies, justice in international trade – fears which then give rise to nationalistic politics. In 2006 we saw an international outcry against the publication of insulting cartoons of the Prophet Mohammed by the Danish press. In this case the advocates of free speech on the one hand and the offended Muslims on the other hand are speaking a different 'language' and using different thought forms. Every country faces issues of social justice, either on a national scale – as seen, for example, in the US Federal Government's response to the devastation caused by Hurricane Katrina in the predominantly poor, black population of New Orleans – or on a local scale. Race, culture, nationality, language, education, wealth, faith, marital status, sexual orientation – all are areas where differences can cause strong feelings leading to passionate arguments and even violence. Sadly, such strong differences also cause divisions within and between churches, so that many Christians cannot or will not share the sacrament of holy communion.

Improvement in world communication resulting from cheap flights, satellite links giving live news coverage, the internet and increases in international trade has actually made us more aware of these differences. So the temptation is to retreat to the familiar, to seek 'people like me'. We prefer to worship in segregated congregations with like-minded people. We become fearful and suspicious of all who are different. Although we are, at one level, conscious that there must be change, deep down we are hoping that the change will merely result in others becoming like us.

This longing for change was actually expressed in a startling way to an archdeacon by members of one PCC in a church of dwindling and elderly membership during an interregnum. Discussing their hopes for a new vicar, they said, 'We know we need to change, and we are prepared for change – as long as it doesn't make any difference to us.' Laughable this may be – but is this not the unspoken longing of so many of us in areas ranging from international politics to our relationship with the person living next door?

The way of the world

Before considering what guidance we can get from the Bible, let us consider various attempts that have been and are being made to handle differences in our multi-cultural, multi-faith and international world.

Segregation

The oppressive and unjust policy of apartheid in South Africa was given theological backing by the Dutch Reformed Church's false belief that black South Africans were created by God as inferior to whites. Fortunately this ended peacefully without the blood-bath that many had feared. In 1990 Nelson Mandela was released after 27 years in prison. In 1994 he became the first democratically elected President of South Africa, whose people he described as a 'rainbow nation'.

Social segregation in Victorian Britain was immortalised by the verse in 'All things bright and beautiful' which is now, thankfully, omitted:[2]

> The rich man in his castle,
> The poor man at his gate,
> He made them, high or lowly,
> And ordered their estate.

The concept of segregation as an official policy may fill us with horror now, but it is a natural human reaction to coping with people who are different. Trevor Phillips, Chair of the Commission for Racial Equality, in a stimulating speech after the 7 July 2005 bombings in London, warned that Britain is 'sleepwalking to segregation': 'The fact is that we are a society which, almost without noticing it, is becoming more divided by race and religion ... It must surely be the most worrying fact of all that younger Britons appear to be integrating less well than their parents.'[3]

Assimilation

No one seriously believes that we should all speak, look, dress, worship and behave in the same way. Yet such assimilation is the hope and expectation of those who advocate the policy of 'when in Rome do as the Romans do'. They would argue that 'If I choose to live in another country I will adopt the customs of that country; so those who come here should adopt our customs.'

The French have attempted a policy of assimilation, and 'to promote the idea of assimilation, neither the State nor any other body publishes statistics on ethnic or national origin.'[4] However, in November 2005 France saw the biggest explosion of street violence since the late 1960s. Seven million residents of Arab and Asian origin felt excluded from the national mainstream. The *Times* commented:

> Three decades on from the big inflow of immigrants, everyone now agrees that the French model has not worked, although almost no one says that the American and British approach has produced better results ... Mainstream Muslim leaders who have been consulted by the Government have all hammered home the message. 'The young have the feeling that they have been abandoned, left at the roadside,' Larbi Kechat, rector of the rue de Tanger mosque in Paris, said.[5]

Integration

Whereas assimilation is a one-way process in which minorities are expected to change and conform to the majority culture, integration is a two-way process whereby, in Trevor Phillips' words, 'The majority accommodates and adopts some of what the minority brings to the party; the minority can be proud of its heritage, even while adapting its ways to be compatible with the majority with whom they now live ... But in a multiethnic society integration doesn't happen without some creative compromises.'[6]

In order to encourage integration and mutual understanding, it has become popular to celebrate diversity by demonstrations of music, dance, clothing or food. However, this emphasises differences rather than those things which unite us.

Legislation

The British Government has introduced an Equality Bill, aiming to outlaw discrimination in the provision of goods and services on the grounds of religion or belief. Discrimination on the grounds of race or disability is already provided for in previous Acts.

The intention is to combat genuine cases of religious discrimination or harassment. However, the fear is that the harassment provisions will create a serious risk to religious freedom – for example, any hospital or university hall of residence which provides Gideon Bibles for patients or students could be accused of breaking the law, as it is claimed this could be potentially offensive to non-Christians.[7]

In a similar way, the Racial and Religious Hatred Bill is an attempt to safeguard British society from the dangers of the extreme fundamentalist who incites hatred on religious grounds. This Bill has been hotly debated. Fortunately, in its amended form it is hard to envisage a case where a Christian, preaching from the word of God in good faith and from good motives, would fall foul of this legislation.

However necessary it may be in practice, legislation is a crude

and ineffective way of achieving integration and racial harmony.
The law cannot force anyone to tolerate or approve of people or
practices they find repugnant.

A biblical view of diversity

Our starting-point must be the doctrine of creation. God created
humankind in his image (Gen. 1:27), both male and female. All
people initially have the same status before God. But after the
fall, we see in God's covenant with Abram (Gen. 12:2–3) that
some people are to be cursed. As God's chosen people entered
the promised land, foreigners or enemies were to be driven out,
defeated, destroyed and shown no mercy, because of their
association with idolatry (Deut. 7:1–6; 1 Kings 11:1–2; Ezra 9:1–2).

But then there is the second group – the sojourner, who was a
settler (Exod. 20:10). The Israelites themselves were sojourners
in Egypt (Exod. 20:10; Gen. 15:13; Exod. 22:13; Deut. 10:19; 23:7) –
so this fact of history was to govern their attitude to sojourners in
Israel. The sojourner had both privileges and responsibilities. He
should not be oppressed (Exod. 22:21; 23:9). God loves the
sojourner, so the Israelites should do the same (Deut. 10:18–19).

Turning to the New Testament, we find first that Jesus radically changes our attitude to the first group above – the stranger,
foreigner or enemy. We are commanded to love not only our
neighbour but also our enemy, and to pray for those who per-
secute us (Matt. 5:43–48). This does not mean being soft on them,
or ignoring sin. God's wrath against the godlessness and wilful
wickedness of humankind continues to be unyielding (Rom.
1:18). Jesus strongly condemned the Pharisees for their hypocrisy
(Matt. 23). God, in his love, wants all to repent (Acts 17:30) and
be saved (1 Tim. 2:4; John 3:17). Jesus commended the faith of an
outsider, the Syro-Phoenician woman (Mark 7:24–30), and freed
her daughter from demon possession. In the parable of the Good
Samaritan he taught that love for one's traditional enemy should
be expressed in practical help at his point of need (Luke 10:33ff).

Paul insists that in Christ human barriers are broken. There is no Jew v. Gentile, slave v. free, male v. female in God's Kingdom, for all have become 'one in Christ' (Gal. 3:28). Paul also reminds those who are Gentile believers that though we were strangers and foreigners to the covenant, we are now no longer aliens. We are fellow citizens (Eph. 2:12, 14–20) with God's people. Yet we journey in this world as pilgrims, chosen to belong not to this world but to the next (John 15:19). We are the ones who are strangers and aliens in this world (1 Pet. 1:7, 17; 2:11).

In the life of the early Church we are given an important example of how to handle differences of belief and practice. The issue facing the Council of Jerusalem (Acts 15) was whether Gentile converts should be required to accept the Mosaic law fully, including circumcision, before they could be saved and welcomed into the Christian Church. This was a very significant stage in the growth of the Church. Four minimum requirements of the law were prescribed – but circumcision was not one of them. This compromise, which must have seemed a painful step too far by some, emerged as the Church's leaders sought God's guidance on a highly controversial matter of doctrine.

Looking to the end times, we see that the blood of Christ 'ransomed for God saints from every tribe and language and people and nation' (Rev. 5:9). John, in his vision, saw 'a great multitude ... from every nation, from all tribes and peoples and languages, standing before the throne' (Rev. 7:9).

The Lee Abbey experience: responses from community members

The Lee Abbey communities in Devon, London, Blackburn, Bristol and Aston come from a variety of backgrounds – national, cultural and denominational. We are male and female, single and married, young and not so young – yet the glue which holds us together is our calling and commitment to seek God, to worship and serve in fellowship together as 'one in Christ'. As an outward expression of this we take community promises, affirming our commitment to Christ, to the community which we join and to service in and through that community.

Does this all sound very 'holy' – almost too good to be true? The words of one past member, three months after she joined the London community, vividly describe the experience that many feel but do not say. A young woman from South Korea, she said:

> Before joining the community I thought it would be wonderful – so many holy people to love me and help me to live like Jesus. But when I came to London I was surprised to see that everyone else is just an ordinary person like me, with human weaknesses. I realised that I have got to be holy before Jesus – and then help others also to be holy. I cannot depend on others. I can only depend on Jesus.

Comments from present and past community members from the various Lee Abbey communities reveal that life in community 'is sometimes viewed by those outside as "unreal" and somehow an easy option – there are all the challenges of life outside community but often intensified because you are living and working together. Any problems have to be worked through but this is also an opportunity for real spiritual growth.'

For most of us in community, our time there is a very positive and enriching experience, especially as an opportunity to get to know people from different backgrounds, cultures and denominations. We learn to 'accept, respect and appreciate the difference between each other'. We 'see people as they are, not as I want them to be'. An older person appreciates 'the vibrancy and challenge of living alongside many much younger people'. Living and working so close together, we have 'to resolve problems (especially relationships) as soon as possible because as a community we can't avoid each other.' It is a 'healthy and safe environment to discover more about yourself and grow spiritually and emotionally.'

But these benefits come with a price. 'Lack of privacy' is the most frequently voiced concern – 'at times I need space to be alone and that is not really possible.' We cannot live independent lives, but have 'to take other people into account when making decisions.' We are brought face to face with the dark side of ourselves ('it shows up more when you're being selfish or difficult') and of others ('some people constantly don't clean up after themselves or have much respect for the fact that others have to live with them'). Difficulties in relationships that arise are not always resolved ('if there are unresolved issues with people, it gets tense, as there is no escape, i.e. everywhere you go they're there').

We grow to understand more about ourselves: 'I'm more accepting of myself – warts and all. God loves me and others do too ... I've learnt to step out and open myself up to make friends easier.' 'You find out more about your gifts, your faults and you have time to work out which way you need to change. There are people around you who help to develop your personality and by this you become stronger and more understandable for others.' We grow towards God: 'knowing God's acceptance of me, freeing me up to be the unique Christian God intends me to be.'

In London, shortage of space means that community volunteers are all in shared rooms – mostly twin but some triple. Often a strong bond of friendship is forged between room-mates, giving mutual support and encouragement. Sometimes this lack of privacy and personal space creates great tension. Some differences may be personal (window open or shut at night; time for going to bed; noise; lights; untidiness; visitors) and some may be cultural (such as the South Korean who used to lie on the floor in the twin room rather than on the bed) – but all such differences require grace and patience to handle in a shared room, which is your only private space. Many of us in community can testify to how God has pruned us (John 15:2) and disciplined us (Heb. 12:4–11) so that we may bear more fruit.

Our community in London has usually included several volunteers from South Africa and also from Eastern Europe. The South Africans, whether black, coloured or white, will have spent their early years under the apartheid regime. The Eastern

Europeans will have spent their early years under commun-
ism, when learning Russian was compulsory in schools, and
Christian teaching and worship had to be either limited and
controlled – or in secret. For them the freedom, the stimulation, the excitement of living, working and worshipping in
London is a joy to behold. One girl from Ukraine, who remem-
bers vividly the time when her country achieved independence
when she was 12 in 1991, wrote from her heart in an Easter
card she gave in 2003:

> Behold, today is the day of the Resurrection. Let us glory in
> this feast, let us embrace one another in joy and say: 'O
> brothers and enemies too: we forgive everything on Res-
> urrection day. Let us all sing together: Christ is risen from
> the dead! He has crushed death by his death and bestowed
> life upon those in the tombs.'

One Hungarian from a Roman Catholic background writes:

> Some of us at Lee Abbey who come from different
> denominations have the strong belief that his/her church
> represents either the most biblical Christian teaching or,
> what is more, the only biblical way of Christian living. I
> also realised here that after studying six years of Roman
> Catholic theology I had a false picture about Christianity. I
> was taught at the university that the only biblical and
> complete way of living was fulfilled in the Catholic Church.
> But at Lee Abbey London I have had the opportunity to get
> to know believers of other Christian denominations whose
> faith and lives made me think and question that teaching.
> Which teaching is more biblical? Which practice fulfils
> better the example Jesus gave us? Mostly we learn from
> these conversations and our opinions are changed. We get
> to know both each other's advantages and weaknesses as
> well, which may make us humble. We need all the
> denominations to reach all the different people with the
> gospel. If we accept each other's differences, which thank

God happens mostly in our community, we can get to know God better and serve him more effectively.

A different reaction comes from a young woman from Ghana with charismatic, Roman Catholic and Methodist past connections, who found the lifestyle of Christians in London one of the biggest challenges:

> It was very strange for me to see Christians in community smoking, tattooing and body piercing and my faith was really challenged but with time I realised that those outside things, though they matter, what really matters is what is in our heart and God sees our heart. And I have had a changed attitude towards such people, loving them just as they are and praying that God makes them see the side-effects of their habits or lifestyle and also the Holy Spirit to bring them out of it.

Another community member, from Latin America, felt that coming to Britain helped her to understand her own culture better. She writes:

> All my experience into a different culture helped me to know my own culture ... There is no better culture; cultures are just different from what each one of us are used to ... Before coming to England ... I learned that England has a history full of war and in some way it affects the culture – people become reserved as a way of protection.

Handling difficult issues

Faith and belief

Opposite the house where we lived in the centre of Lahore was a large hostel for medical students. I have often wondered how I would have reacted if I had been a student at the University of the Punjab in Lahore, residing in one of the student halls of residence. This has been a helpful model in guiding some of the decisions at Lee Abbey International Students' Club, where we have 150 students of any faith or none, and for whom this is their home during their studies – a 'home-from-home', as we advertise.

I would expect the hostel to be predominantly Muslim, with perhaps one or two Christian Pakistani students to reflect the two per cent of Christians in the population as a whole. I would expect the life of the hostel to be clearly adapted to a Muslim lifestyle – for example, giving time and place for those who wished to be regular in their daily prayers, and changing the meal times during the month of Ramadan to enable students to fast during the hours of daylight. I would be neither surprised nor offended to see a copy of the Quran placed beside each bedside.

I would expect to see Muslim art and architecture evident throughout the building. I would expect some of the fellow students to take an intelligent yet respectful interest in my Christian beliefs – even perhaps trying to convince me that Islam was the only true religion. None of these would cause me any offence. However, what would cause offence would be if I was expected to enter into any of the Muslim practices, or if I was regarded as a second-class student because I was not Muslim, or if Christian symbols, belief or practice were mocked or insulted. The key issue is respect for me as a person, and for my beliefs, as long as they do not conflict with the local majority in a practical or moral way. I would hope for a lifestyle in the hostel which enables people of strongly held yet conflicting religious beliefs to live alongside each other with mutual respect.

Translating this hypothetical situation back into British society – sometimes we have been too apologetic, too afraid of causing offence and unnecessarily conscious of 'political correctness'.

Inter-faith and lifestyle issues

Lee Abbey London, though run by a resident Christian community, is home to students of all faiths and none. It is significant to compare the experience of the student hostel with the situation in the multi-racial, multi-faith area of Aston, the site of the Lee Abbey community house. Students are away from home and the pressures of family, concentrating on their studies, and usually open to new ideas and ways of thinking. Student culture is almost a separate culture in itself, with the students developing an awareness of other cultures which loosens their ties with their country of origin and their religious traditions. Many, after graduation, look for jobs in London rather than returning to their own countries. Inter-faith dialogue in such a situation is a minority interest. In the last few years two events have triggered a communal inter-faith spiritual response. The first was the 9/11 terrorist attacks in New York in 2001, when the chapel was opened to all for quiet prayer. The second was in March 2002 when Aymar Yao, a student from Ivory Coast, died of sickle-cell anaemia, and we had a memorial service in the chapel.

In contrast to the situation in the London student hostel, the people of Aston tend to live in social groups with people from their own faith or ethnic background. There are the Muslim Pakistanis and Bangladeshis (each with their own mosque), and the Christian Afro-Caribbeans. Personal and group progress depends on mutual support within each group. The natural tendency for each group is to seek security – whether of jobs, property, schooling, or social activities – within one's own group. This creates a problem for the second generation who are students in a Western world, yet still living in their own culture at home. Older people, especially in the mosques, fear that their children will lose their culture as they are absorbed into the Western educational system. There is great tension between the generations, with the children often living two separate lives, unable to reconcile the differences between life at home and life at college with their peers.

Within this situation the Lee Abbey Household community in Aston tries to build relations with local families, seeking to respect, accept and understand both parents and their children. Members of the community work with local people – in the schools or the advice centre. The mere fact that they also live in the same area generates respect, in contrast to so many professionals working in Aston who live outside in more comfortable and affluent areas. The Household community share food at Christmas or Eid, Ramadan or Easter. The Christian Justice and Peace Group sent a card of greetings to the mosques during One World Week. With the friendships comes mutual trust: 'when you are friends with someone of another culture, you are concerned for their well-being, and they for yours.' Such friends stand together – whether this is against terrorism and violence or in helping the young people to form healthy and pure relationships with no sex before marriage.

Such friendships were stretched to the limit during the Afghanistan and Iraq wars. In some Asian shops the community members were clearly not welcome – even though these shopkeepers were their friends. Being in the Lee Abbey house with other Christians enabled each to live more healthily, securely and prayerfully, with stability and without anxiety. This is especially evident at crisis times, when there are riots, and guns on the street. Residence in the Lee Abbey house, as a place of prayer, has enabled the community members to be present as a resource for local people and not as a drain.

Moral issues

One of the issues we have had to face at Lee Abbey London relates to personal morals. We are a mixed hostel, with a roughly equal number of male and female students. We have had to think very carefully about how we handle issues of sexual morality. As a Christian community we have clear guidelines about such issues within the community. However, for the students, for whom this is home just as much as it is for the community, we have to allow freedom as long as their behaviour does not affect others. We naturally insist that shared rooms are single sex unless the couple is married. We also have a rule that no one should stay overnight in a room they are not booked into. We have guidelines about not causing offence or embarrassment:

Private morality is an individual concern. However, the laws about such matters as racism and sexual harassment are strong in Britain. We have a responsibility to enable everyone to live here without being subjected to the pressures of permissive behaviour, which can cause offence. Standards of morality at Lee Abbey are those which are traditional in many other cultures. Just as we expect high standards of honesty and integrity, we also expect tolerance and respect for other cultures. We need to be sensitive and avoid undermining others by saying hurtful things, or making jokes that could be misunderstood and cause offence. Please avoid language and behaviour and dress that may embarrass those from different cultures than your own. This includes any physical display of affection that might be misunderstood or embarrass others.[8]

What happens, then, if one of our House Team in their weekly cleaning of a student bedroom has reason to believe that a couple of students are in bed together during the day? The students know which day their room will be cleaned; we observe their privacy by knocking three times on the door and respond within reason to repeated requests to 'come back later'. But they are adults, and while we may disapprove of some activities of some students, we have to respect their personal freedom as long as it does not contravene the carefully worded rules or cause embarrassment.

This principle has implications in our wider relationship with those who are different. We can and do sit in judgement on those whose different beliefs result in action that is plainly wrong. An extreme example of this is the terrorist or the suicide bomber. Although it is often said that 'one man's terrorist is another man's freedom fighter', nevertheless violence which involves random and indiscriminate attacks on the lives of innocent civilians is clearly the wrong way to settle a dispute. But if the action of those who have different beliefs is neither morally wrong, nor socially unacceptable, then we have to find a way to live alongside such differences in harmony.

Denominational issues

The Lee Abbey community is not a church, nor do we pretend to be one. In fact, in the London community we have no worship in chapel on Sundays, so that community members can worship in a local church of their choice. Whether Pentecostal, Roman Catholic, Methodist, Orthodox, Baptist, Anglican, or Coptic – we live and worship as 'one in Christ'. Such a denomination-ally mixed community is an ideal place to learn about other churches – and some value the opportunity to discuss theo-logical issues such as the place of women in the Church, the importance of Mary in our faith, or the influence of the Holy Spirit on our lives and in our worship.

Apart from our daily worship each weekday, our central act of worship is the Wednesday holy communion when we express our unity in Christ by sharing the bread and wine around the Lord's table together. But this inevitably raises the question of intercommunion – should we welcome into the community those from Roman Catholic or Orthodox churches who cannot openly share with us the body and blood of Christ?[9]

Lessons applied

What conclusions, then, can we draw from the Lee Abbey experience of community which may be of help in general to Christians in our relationship with those who are different in some way?

The first essential is to see each individual as precious, created in God's image. When Samuel was sent to choose the future king of Israel, God said to him: 'the Lord does not see as mortals see; they look on the outward appearance, but the Lord looks on the heart.'[10] This is not easy when we see something we do not understand, or which we believe to be morally wrong.

Secondly, there must be a desire or willingness to build a relationship across the divide. This willingness can only have any meaning if we are dealing with a relationship with people whom we meet on a reasonably regular basis. Listening, understanding, relating is a two-way process – and any progress must depend on the willingness of the other person to reciprocate. Our experience of living in community has born out the obvious fact that we must make an effort to relate – and people do respond when we take the initiative, since they know that they are being valued.

We must recognise that this willingness to relate also means that we risk being hurt – we are vulnerable. Anyone, for example, who is involved in inter-faith dialogue must make themselves vulnerable. Roger Hooker, reporting on his years of inter-faith dialogue with Hindus in India, writes about a 'rediscovery of friendship'. Communication is an 'art that has to be learnt'. Through communication we make the 'humiliating, painful and very necessary discovery' of 'how strange and incomprehensible other people find our language, our customs, our beliefs'.[11] The person who never sees a black face in rural England, and prides himself that he is 'not racist', can say this easily and may be completely honest in this assertion. But because he is not vulnerable, he has not begun to realise the complexity of the situation. If I am in such a situation, I should ask myself, 'How do I relate to the person next door, or across the road, who lives a completely different lifestyle?' The commandment we have from Christ is this: those who love God must love their brothers and sisters also.[12]

Thirdly, be prepared to differ in love. An extreme example of this is the situation where a husband and wife worship in different churches – or perhaps one worships regularly but the other does not – and yet they give mutual encouragement and support to each other in their different beliefs without compromising their own.

I believe that we can affirm the uniqueness of Jesus Christ as the only Lord, God and Saviour, while at the same time admitting humbly that our knowledge and understanding of God is limited.[13] We all need an intellectual humility and an awareness that no one can know the whole truth about God in this life. There is always more to learn, and sometimes this means letting go of cherished beliefs. An example of this occurred when I was in Bristol Diocese in 1992, at the time of the final voting by General Synod for the Church of England to ordain women to the priesthood. I remember with great respect one member of the local clergy chapter who said, 'I am opposed to the ordination of women to the priesthood. But there has been much prayer and debate about this over the years – and if the church's representatives in Synod vote to ordain women as priests, then I shall have to accept that decision as God's guidance, and therefore that my current belief is mistaken.'

NOTES

1. Text installed on the North Wall of Trafalgar Square, commissioned by Events for London, funded by the *International Herald Tribune*.
2. Although in the 1990s I was horrified to see this verse printed in the Order of Service at a wedding at which I was officiating. On the assumption that most people do not think about what they are singing, I decided not to draw attention to the error – and merely stopped singing for that verse.
3. Trevor Phillips, 'After 7/7: Sleepwalking to Segregation', speech on 22 November 2005 to the Manchester Council for Community Relations.
4. *TimesOnLine*, 7 November 2005, 'Colour-blind policy has fed Muslim radicalism'.
5. Ibid.
6. Trevor Phillips, 'Equality in our Lifetime', CRE press release, 28 October 2005.
7. Andrea Williams, Public Policy Officer of the Lawyers' Christian Fellowship, 28 October 2005.
8. 'Information and Rules for Residents at Lee Abbey International Students' Club', p. 16.
9. This issue is referred to in Chapter 4, 'Community and Worship'.
10. 1 Sam. 16:7.
11. Roger Hooker, *Voices of Varanasi* (CMS, 1979), p. 12.
12. See 1 John 4:20–21: 'Those who say, "I love God," and hate their brothers or sisters, are liars; for those who do not love a brother or sister whom they have seen, cannot love God whom they have not seen.'
13. For further reading see, for example, Chris Wright, *The Uniqueness of Jesus* (Monarch Books, 1997).

7

Mike Edson

COMMUNITY AND
CONFLICT

*Ven. Mike Edson was Warden of Lee Abbey Devon from 1989 to 1994.
On leaving Lee Abbey he became Archdeacon of Leicester and Diocesan
Evangelist. He is now the Bideford Team Rector of the Torridge
Estuary Team. He is the author of* The Renewal of the Mind *(Hodder
and Stoughton, 1988) and* Loved into Life *(Marshall Pickering,
1983).*

Historically the Church, both local and international, has a
dubious record on its success in handling conflict, yet the New
Testament boldly tells of the conflict between Paul and Peter as
to how non-Jewish Christians should be treated, and Paul
showed no hesitation in venting his frustration with the false
apostles who were damaging the faith of the newly founded
churches in Corinth and Galatia. Regrettably, though, Church
history is littered with division, the Reformation being a clear
example, division caused by conflict over different interpreta-
tions of the Bible, authority and church order. These days it

appears that church conflict is generally resolved by one group or another forming its own understanding of what it is to be church; some cannot accept women in leadership, others gay people, others the central place of the Bible. So they split off and become a 'new church'. Given that Christian history is somewhat chequered, what can the Lee Abbey experience of community offer modestly to the Church at large? Does it have a culture that can be helpful to other communities of people?

Culture

Culture is difficult to define. Even the best sociological books can only offer, 'It is what is expected of us'. Culture is what soaks into our souls and minds, predisposing us as to how to carry on the purpose of the organisation to which we belong. Conflicts arise within organisations and human relationships, so how conflict is handled will depend on their culture or cultures. For example, recent history in Northern Ireland had, in some sections of the Protestant and Catholic communities, created a 'culture of violence' as the means to resolve community difficulties. Other nationalities, particularly in the East, have created a culture where saving face takes priority in behaviour, and facing conflict openly may well be avoided.

However, cultures do not simply spring into existence. There is a period of formation, during which there are recognisable characteristics which both create and maintain those cultures. These are primarily the routines, customs, rituals and stories that a community tells itself. Sometimes it can happen that where two sub-cultures are in opposition, they might hold quite different stories and rituals about a common historical event that affected both. The question is whether it is possible to create a culture that intends to resolve conflict creatively and what routines, customs, rituals and stories might be needed to do that.

The Lee Abbey culture

Rituals: the joining ceremony

This is an important process for new members joining the community. Beginning with a probation period of three months or so, fresh members can observe and be observed. There is some basic training about becoming a member, practical spiritual disciplines, and grasping the vision of the purpose of Lee Abbey's work. Only when the leadership is content that new members have a reasonable grasp of that vision, and these members are ready to work for it, are they allowed to leave their probationary period and become full members.

This initial time is crucial for the welfare of the community. The local church might itself benefit if it had a way of orientating new members to understand the vision and purpose that God has for it in its locality. Of course, that means the local church has to seek what God wants of it first, and that has to be part of the life-blood of the church. Not surprisingly, where there is no vision, no overarching understanding and accepted common purpose, factions and groups arise pursuing differing agendas, and unnecessary conflict will invariably result. Some churches that have been to Lee Abbey Devon on weekends away have explored the possibility of adopting an equivalent of the Lee Abbey community promises as a source of shared vision for their church communities.

How does your church or organisation initiate new members into accepting its vision?

Rituals: the commitment ceremony

After the probationary period, the new member stands before the rest of the community to make extensive promises. One promise in particular focuses on the culture formed over the decades that helps to manage conflict:

> Are you prepared to live in fellowship, being open to be known for who you are, accepting one another in Christ,

and saying of others nothing that could not be said to them personally if love and wisdom required it?

Of course, echoes of the substance of that promise can be found in the New Testament (Phil. 2:1–4), and hopefully Christians fashion their lives accordingly, but there needs to be a positive effort to create that sort of culture. Personal declarations made before other members of a church or community create a supportive structure helping to maintain and further an ethos of behaviour and attitude. Such declarations state how members will behave towards one another. This means they can be called into account by other members of the community when expectations are broken.

However, these promises are aspirations, and it would be dishonest to claim that gossip, and at times, malicious gossip, does not occur. Nevertheless, community formation and enrichment of culture develops by testing against the benchmark provided by the promises. It is a fundamental 'court of appeal' when difficulty in relationships arise.

Stories

Rituals and stories embrace, enhance and reinforce the culture of any group, whether it is a Lee Abbey community, an international business or a family – even stories about how conflict was handled.

There has to be a place and time for such story-telling. In Lee Abbey this happens especially at the weekly community meeting. Business is transacted; base is touched; but one important part is 'the leaving speech' given by members about to depart. The departing community member will tell the story of what they have learned and achieved over their time in community. Sometimes the story tells of skills learned, creative abilities discovered, new vision of God and, invariably, challenging lessons learned through their interaction with guests and other community members. Other members recall stories of former members, so past and present entwine. However, such sharing of experiences can only happen as the community members have learned to be sensitive to both their own and others' emotional reactions, sometimes in difficult circumstances. And it is this lesson well learned which creates an enhanced ability to deal with conflict.

Routines

Learning to be sensitive to emotional needs and reactions in others and ourselves requires a degree of self-knowledge, particularly how we desire to create an environment around us in which we feel 'at home'. The Greek word for 'home' is *ecos* (*oikos*), which is the root of words such as 'economy' and 'ecology', meaning how we bring order to where we live and how we study it.

Yet 'at home' has a powerful meaning within itself. It is not merely the environment we create, but the expectations on ourselves and others as to how we behave and how things should be done. We carry this understanding of 'feeling at home' with us. It is a powerful expression of our ego; our ego uses its power, creates for itself an environment in which it feels reasonably at peace with itself. I remember a musician who had recently joined the community, playing the piano extremely loudly for two or three months: 'Here I am. Here is who I am. You will notice me!'

Obviously it is highly unlikely that any group of individuals share the same *ecos*, and conflict will arise when there is a clash between them. At times this can degenerate into a power struggle for dominance, for even in a Christian community no one's ego has been totally transformed by the love of God. We need to learn how to live together, how to understand one another, how (using an over-used phase) we 'communicate with one another'.

The great benefit of the various methods of discerning different personality types, such as the Myers Briggs or Enneagram systems, is that they help us understand why others can be incredibly difficult and irritating much of the time, and why they find us the same. People are remarkably different, and the skill of sensitivity training is not only being able to step into the shoes of another person and attempt to understand the way they think and behave, but also to begin to see how that person perceives how we, in turn, think and behave the way we do.

One of the great lessons I learned living in the Lee Abbey community was the truth behind an old saying: 'Your enemy is your soul's best friend.' Your 'enemy' will soon reveal unresolved negative thoughts and desires within your soul which need the Lord's attentive work.

Realising why people are different is an important part of the process, and necessary to commence sensitivity training. The other ongoing process is learning communication and listening skills, without which destructive conflict is more likely to happen.

This entails a training process using material from relationship enrichment courses, such as marriage enrichment and basic counselling courses, with an intended objective of giving individuals the freedom and ability to speak what they are feeling and thinking about themselves, others and situations, and the ability and experience to listen to and understand others.

Such sensitivity training depends on the building of mutual trust and confidentiality between people and groups. This is more than dialogue; it is a mutual sharing and listening about concerns and issues. Of course, sensitivity training is far more than dealing with possible conflict areas; mutual sharing is also more about encouraging each other to advance the vision of the group.

Opportunity for being with others is needed for this depth of sharing to develop. It does not happen automatically in Lee Abbey, simply because people are living together. Relationship building has to be energised in the fabric of the community, church or any institution. In fact, experts of Management and Organisation Behaviour for industry and commerce advocate sensitivity training. Many churches move in this direction by the formation of home groups or cells, where mutual listening and sharing are encouraged.

Having understood how culture is formed, how will this help us to handle conflict?

The causes of conflict

Everyone creates an *ecos*, a personal way of living, of accommodation in which we feel at home. It is an outward expression of the power we have over our immediate environment, how we arrange our furniture, and how we create an atmosphere where we also are emotionally, socially and intellectually comfortable and 'at home' with ourselves.

So what happens when we meet others who, by the nature of humanity, do not share in or want to take part in our *ecos*, because they have already made their own comfortable home? People can and do, of course, avoid one another and go their separate ways, bouncing off one another like billiard balls. 'Who could possibly live with him!' But what happens if we have to share the same living space? In marriage it is love which is the supporting energy given to a couple to come to a living arrangement, but in a community, church or other organisation, such emotion and commitment is not necessarily the given, and hard times may come as differing requirements clash. Whose view, whose power will ultimately predominate? Is there a way of developing a common *ecos* which all parties will own?

In the first round of the tussle, there are usually four presenting causes of conflict, all to do with creating our own 'at home'. These are: conflict over power; conflict over resources; conflict over direction; conflict over status. These are the arms and legs for wrestling to construct our own *modus vivendi*.

Power issues
These are about asserting our own egos. I want to do what you are doing. I want to be in charge, I want my ideas to prevail. Power bids are made by asserting our ideas, attempting to take control of the group, the community, the church council. It can be done subtly or aggressively. It can take the form of creating a

'gang' to take control over the organisation. Regrettably, a significant number of clergy dread attending the meeting of their church councils, since they know they will once again be entering a conflict arena.

The wise-heads at national archdeacons' conferences recognise wryly those who want to be bishops by the frequency with which they stand up in public meetings and put their views. Variations of this are found in some marriages, where power struggles can undermine the relationship.

Resource issues

These are based primarily around wanting to have what others have. Sometimes there is a genuine case for justice and fairness in distributing resources. Some of the problems regarding financial allowances in Lee Abbey were resolved by everyone in the community receiving the same allowance, dependent on their length of service. The Church of England tackled the problem of rich and poor livings by taking over the income from land (glebe) and giving all clergy the same stipend.

The problem arises especially where there is a shortage of resources; and competition arises where individuals or groups make bids as to why their need is greater than anyone else's. Some of the most difficult problems at Lee Abbey Devon in the past have arisen because of the lack of suitable accommodation for single mature women, and for families. The potential for grievances when someone who had more recently joined the community jumped the queue was, understandably, extremely high. How can we deal with conflict when resources remain limited?

Status issues

These are to do with the need to be recognised as someone of importance and significance by the group. This might be an assumed expert on cooking for the guests; on prayer ministry; on getting the chapel ready for communion. In the local church they might be those who lead small groups, or arrange the flowers, or organise an aspect of church life. These are the positions in which people find their identity and, of course, conflict will be likely if others, even leaders, overrun these responsibilities or ignore them.

How many times have you felt offended by someone taking over your job or your position?

Direction issues

These are to do with wanting the relationship, the group, the community to go the way I want it to. In the past direction issues have been raised as to which way the Lee Abbey movement should go. Should it, in the 1950s, go the way of providing 'home from home' accommodation in London for overseas students? No doubt deep discussions and debate arose at that time about this.

Should Lee Abbey Devon be providing small-holding facilities and husbandry of animals? Were we a farm or a centre for Christian renewal? How should we behave in the community kitchen? Should the washing up be left to dry or should it be dried with a tea-towel? Little problems? Most of the hippy communities in the 1970s disbanded not over ideology, but over practicalities such as that.

Inadequate ways of resolving conflict

There are at least five inadequate strategies or stances by which conflict appears to have been resolved. These are avoidance, non-cooperation, submission, collaboration and third-party force.

Avoidance

Many people find conflict difficult and disturbing, so a convenient way is to avoid those situations where conflict is likely to arise. Meetings can be missed, and when there is no choice but to meet the other person, we do not mention or talk about any problems that might cause difficulty. Perhaps the other person is too touchy; perhaps we fear what might be said to us. Perhaps if nothing is said, the problem will simply dissipate over time. Of course, this strategy may well be the right one in some circumstances; it can be wise to let sleeping dogs lie, but that is different from an attitude which avoids all conflict.

Some of the major challenges facing the worldwide Anglican Communion are differing views regarding homosexuality and women priests and bishops. It is difficult not to come to some preliminary conclusions about the first. For many years avoidance seemed to be the tactic commonly used, even if it was disguised as 'turning a blind eye'.

If that is true for the international Church, it is also true for the local church. Significant challenges may be made to the leadership, unbiblical lifestyles may be openly displayed. But how tempting to avoid the conflict in the hope that 'they' will go away. The boat must not be rocked.

The truth is, no deep relationship – whether in church, community or family – will form until there is a way of facing conflict constructively.

Non-cooperation
Those who have brought up teenagers are familiar with this approach. Non-cooperation is a tactic by which we might give the impression we are in full or part agreement with what is suggested, but in reality our resolve is not to cooperate at all. Of course, this is not solely a teenage tactic. I have attended local government meetings where the chairperson has appealed to council members that, once they have agreed on a policy or a course of action at the meeting, they really should not go to the press with an alternative, criticising the agreed decision. An appeal from bitter, embarrassing experience! Non-cooperation in this way is subversive and divisive and is likely to lead to tremendous tensions and destructive conflict.

Submission
In the case of submission, people simply give up and surrender to the powerful people in the relationship. 'If that's what you

want – OK, have your own way!' They may deeply resent what is happening, but feel totally powerless and have no choice but to do what is expected of them. In times of high unemployment and financial insecurity, ruthless employers may·well use their power over those who work for them. I know of an employer in the 1930s who sacked the slowest worker every week – an obvious abuse of power over those who had no power to protest.

There are, sadly, many examples of abuse in marital relationships where one of the partners dominates the other physically and/or emotionally, where the submissive one feels totally helpless. Surrendering or giving up to the domineering power within a group fails to challenge the ego-power of the dominator.

Collaboration

This may be a staging-post to true co-operation, since at its best, two or more parties are prepared to lay aside their differences and collaborate on a common task or concern. This will work reasonably well until there is a clash over what has been laid aside – the non-negotiable areas.

Politically, mediators work hard to establish collaboration between parties whose views are radically opposed to one another. Where there is little hope of collaboration, there is not much chance of success. Churches of different denominations often need long periods of collaboration on projects common to both before they become confident to tackle the differences that give them their distinctiveness. Anglican culture, its *ecos*, is in many ways different from, say, Baptist culture and its *ecos*.

The worst example of collaboration happens when individuals or groups join the most powerful group or person in the organisation. This can mean the collaborator has surrendered any personal view and absorbed the outlook of the group. Teenage groups come to mind. At other times, the collaborator may be playing a waiting game and may attempt eventually to add their own agenda to the group.

Third-party force

This is sometimes called 'the United Nations option'. When two or more opposing factions are in bitter dispute, then a stronger third party enters the situation and enforces peace by keeping the parties apart and attempting to make them negotiate.

There is a peace, in the sense that there is an absence of open hostility, but the danger is that the causes of conflict may be unaddressed, and in world history that grievance may be hundreds of years old. The test is what happens when the third party withdraws.

These five ways of dealing with conflict may each, in their various methods, present a superficial appearance of peace, but really it is just the absence of open conflict. It is as the Old Testament declares: ' "Peace, peace," they say, when there is no peace' (Jer. 6:14).

Biblical ways of resolving conflict

Self-examination

The first step is *self-examination* (Matt. 7:1–5). Being aware that someone in the group or community is causing us a problem is not in itself sufficient reason to speak to that person about it.

Self-examination is required, particularly looking at the force and power of the 'myth' we might have of the other. No one can ever comprehend another person fully, since it is hard enough to do that for ourselves. Instead we receive impressions of the other from what they say and how they behave, and from those impressions we create a picture, an image, a 'myth' of who they are. From that myth we make predictions as to what they are thinking and how they will behave. As long as relationships are content and congenial, this presents no problem to us, but if the other person behaves badly, our 'myth' of them is in danger of changing in a negative way, and we believe that this new myth is the real person. Problems lie ahead when we begin to behave according to that new myth, and the danger is that we will be deaf to hearing anything that might change our picture. Consequently self-examination works at many levels.

We need to ask ourselves, 'Am I behaving and responding towards the other person according to my myth of them? Are they behaving and responding according to the myth they have of me?' Sometimes another person who is not directly involved might help us to come to a clearer picture of the situation.

It is well known that someone with whom we are in conflict might well be showing us areas in our own lives to which we are blind and which require some prayerful attention. 'Your enemy is your soul's best friend.'

First of all, we must attend to the beam in our own eye before criticising the splinter in someone else's. Honesty, prayerfulness, a cool head and a forgiving self-assessment are needed.

Obtain the facts

The second step is *obtain the facts*. St Paul had to deal with a significant problem of sexual immorality in the Corinthian church. In 1 Corinthians 5:1 and 6:1–6 he indicated that he was totally aware of the facts: 'It is actually reported that there is sexual immorality among you.'

In my own experience it is not uncommon to make too many false assumptions about the reason why others have behaved or acted in certain ways. I call it the 'peas-on-the-hob' syndrome, discovered when I noticed certain people leaving church when I was speaking. 'What have I said to offend them? Are they really converted?' All sorts of assumptions and inappropriate judgements went through my mind. In fact, they had left because they had remembered that they needed to turn off the oven! The danger is that we create an unhelpful myth about other people – unhelpful in that it might predispose us to treat them with suspicion, indifference or even hostility.

Some years ago a dispute arose concerning responsibility for the development of the Lee Abbey buildings. Did the responsibility rest ultimately with the Holding Trustees, or with the Lee Abbey Council? This was no small matter, but it was the facts obtained by objective legal opinion that resolved a difficult situation between the two bodies. It is therefore crucial to discover the facts as to why a problem arose, when it happened and the truth of the situation.

This is especially important where individuals or others have the responsibility of dealing with complaints about behaviour between two parties or individuals. It is a regrettable feature of human life that parties in grievance will tend to emphasise that part of the truth that supports their case and play down that part which does not! Nevertheless, even in such cases, each party's story must be noted and agreed before 'judgement' can be given. There have been several situations of conflict between members of community at Lee Abbey where it has been essential for a person in a leadership role to talk to both parties (sometimes together) to find out the facts of the situation.

Speaking the truth in love

The third step is *speaking the truth in love* (Eph. 4:15). This verse gives no one sanction to discharge their views and feelings to a brother or sister in Christ. The right attitude is one that desires a good outcome that is beneficial to both parties, one that desires the welfare of the other as well as ourselves. Such an attitude of 'treating the other in the same way we would like ourselves to be treated' shapes and forms what we say and how we will say it.

A meeting needs to be set up. It may take several, depending on the depth and nature of the issues causing conflict. The received wisdom from relationship-building is to address the problem in ways that present the facts and enable us to express our own feeling and thoughts about our perception of what has taken place. In other words, we resist the temptation to accuse the other of creating any negative emotions we might feel. Our feelings are self-generated, and the cause may well lie solely within us. That is precisely what needs to be discerned. The meeting will have these characteristics:

- It will not accuse the other of creating anything negative or disruptive.
- We will express how we feel when we see the other behaving or speaking in a certain manner.
- The other, whether an individual or a group, will listen attentively, only interrupting for clarification, with the purpose of trying to understand why the speaker has the feelings they have.
- The first speaker will then be silent and listen to what the other has to say.

This cycle is done in the spirit of Ephesians 4:32: 'Be kind and compassionate to one another, forgiving each other just as God in Christ forgave you.' This can be difficult, but both parties must resist the temptation to let negative feelings shape their words. With grace and mutual charity, a living arrangement may be achieved through this process, and at best an agreed consensus and a change in behaviour by both parties might well result.

This process will also work for groups in conflict, although it is more difficult. When groups are in conflict, the danger is that negative feelings about the other group can become more dominant than any charitable disposition. Group dynamics can reduce the sensitivities of the individuals who make up the group. Each group will need a suitable spokesperson. Invariably someone needs to act as a convenor/mediator to ensure that the groups keep to the characteristics mentioned above and to stimulate the groups to consider the position of those with whom they disagree.

Last resorts

The fourth step, and the last resort, is to take witnesses (Matt. 18:15–17). In this reading, Jesus instructed his followers to meet individually with others in the first place, but what if someone refuses to be reconciled, and what if they continue to be destructive to the community? Witnesses are then needed. However, this fourth step must only take place when the

individuals' face-to-face meetings have failed to resolve the difficulty and where there is a genuine problem and grievance in
hand.

What is unacceptable is when someone is confronted with the
problem without warning in the presence of others who are not
involved. It is likely that the aggrieved person will be using the
others for their own support, using them as witnesses for their
cause, even deliberately putting the other at a disadvantage. Not
surprisingly, this is a sure recipe for deeper hostility. If this is the
motive for bringing in witnesses, even deeper self-examination
needs to take place and facts need to be verified.

The other parties are witnesses to the truth of the facts and to
the integrity of the meeting. They are not chosen to back up those
who are feeling threatened or aggrieved. They are there to dis-
cern the truth so that both sides may be changed accordingly. It
is 'the truth which sets us free'. These meetings continue as long
as there is any possibility of the conflict being resolved, and are
private and confidential.

Only as the final resort, where the conflict is irresolvable and
the issues concerned could cause disruption to the group or
community, should those who lead that group be involved.
These leaders then act as arbiters, hearing both sides and
deciding on a course of action. But sadly, there will be rare
occasions when disruptive individuals may be required to leave,
and there have been such cases in the London and Devon
communities. Such action always causes great regret and
distress.

The process of listening attentively and being able to speak our
innermost thoughts in confidence is necessary for establishing
deep relationships, not only in a community like Lee Abbey, but
in any group. In this way conflict can be used to deepen relationships rather than damage them.

8

Chris Edmondson

COMMUNITY AND LEADERSHIP

Revd Chris Edmondson has been Warden of Lee Abbey Devon since 2002. Following ordination in 1973, he has worked in a variety of Anglican parish and diocesan posts. He is the author of a number of books on leadership and mission, including Fit to Lead *(DLT, 2002).*

Developing emerging leaders

When asked what he would do if he knew he was going to die the next day, the Reformation leader Martin Luther replied, 'I would plant a tree.' Allied to this observation, I am reminded of a folk proverb: 'The best time to plant a tree was 20 years ago. The second best time is now.'

This analogy of tree planting seems to me to be a helpful metaphor to describe the process of developing leaders for today's Church and world. New leaders *may* emerge, whether those responsible do anything about it or not. But the quality and usefulness of new leaders, like trees, is usually enhanced when we are intentional about the task – something the Church has generally not been good at – the task being to ensure they are positively cultivated, pruned where necessary, nourished and well placed. Churches that have a vision for effective leadership in the days ahead are cultivating emerging leaders now. The best time would have been to start 20 years ago, but the second best time is now.

As is so often the case, it seems it is a crisis that is forcing the Church to get to grips with this issue. With notable exceptions, most of the mainstream denominations find themselves with ageing congregations and a smaller 'paid workforce' whose average age is higher than it was 20 years ago. There is the recognition that if something radical does not happen, some of the gloomy predictions of recent surveys, that question whether or not the future will have a Church, could well come true. Thankfully, there are some signs of fresh commitment to a process of 'tree-planting' and, as I will illustrate, this is something to which Lee Abbey has been committed since its inception in 1946.

My own commitment to cultivating especially young, emerging leaders has its roots in my own calling and experience, because, even though the term was not used then, I was once what would now be called an 'emerging leader'! I was selected for ordination into the Church of England at the age of 20 and was ordained at 23. After a six-year curacy, I was appointed as Vicar of a challenging urban parish. Seven years later, in my mid thirties, I was entrusted with the responsibility of being a Diocesan Missioner. Whether there was a particular point at which I 'emerged', I do not know, but over the last 20 years, whether in the context of the local church, or Lee Abbey, or other opportunities I have been given, it has been a privilege to be involved in discerning and developing the potential of emerging leaders.

This latter period of time also coincides with having a greater clarity as to how the leadership gift expresses itself, and how that potential can be discerned and developed. There are many different ways of defining what we mean by 'leadership', and I have written elsewhere in more detail on this subject.[1] However, core to everything is understanding that there is a distinctive spiritual gift of leadership. This has not always been recognised and understood by the Church at large. Ministry and leadership often seem to get confused. St Paul, however, writing to the church in Rome, in the course of describing the variety of gifts given to the Church, says, 'if it [i.e. your gift] is leadership, you are to govern diligently' (Rom. 12:8). In other words, he is urging the men and women who have been entrusted with leadership gifts to take them seriously, to develop them fully, and to deploy them as appropriate, so that they can enable people with other gifts to work together to make a difference in the world.

To summarise what this gift 'looks like', I believe the leadership gift and calling is expressed in two key ways: *giving direction* and *developing people*. If this understanding is right, two other things need to follow. First of all, there needs to be a *vision* for leadership development. In my experience, whether in the local church or somewhere like Lee Abbey, the greatest obstacle to this is the pressure of immediate and urgent demands. These crowd out time and diminish energy for thinking ahead as to where the church or organisation is going, and who and where the leaders are to be found who can give direction, and in turn develop others. This will always slip to the bottom of the agenda unless those currently in leadership intentionally keep it at the top.

It has been rightly said that in most churches 10 per cent of the congregation can take up 90 per cent of the leaders' time. The problem is, they are not the 10 per cent to whom we should be giving so much time! If I have any regrets, looking back over 30 years of ministry, it is that I have not given sufficient time to such leadership development.

Apparently, on John Wesley's gravestone in London is the inscription, 'God burns his workmen, but his work goes on.' For those of us who currently have leadership responsibilities, this perspective of equipping others to go further and do better than we have done shows that we have begun to understand something of this vision, and the legacy we can thereby leave.

However, vital as it is, creating such a vision is only the first step. The second challenge is to develop a *strategy* that turns that vision into a reality. One of the ways this happens begins with spotting people's potential. Taking Lee Abbey as an example, this can take a number of forms. If, as I believe it is, leadership is about the capacity to influence others, rather than looking for particular leadership traits, I want to ask instead, 'What is happening to others as a result of that person's influence?' If they are responsible for a small group, is the group enthusiastic? Are they learning? Is the group growing? Thus, someone in the community might emerge as having leadership gifts in a small-group context, who is then given the opportunity to assist in the leadership of a team responsible for a church weekend. If that proves successful, they may be asked to take responsibility for planning and leading a week-long team in the programme. Similarly, I have seen people show potential for leadership in one of our work-teams – for example, the estate, youth or the kitchen – and when a vacancy occurs they rise to the challenge of responsibility for its leadership.

One 18-year-old, taking a gap before university at Lee Abbey, Devon, found that the experience of a year living in community was profoundly formative, providing experience of teamwork and leadership in the context of a Christian community. That experience proved to be a significant thread in a life tapestry that led to his becoming the Chief Executive of a major Christian publishing house, and later, a Diocesan Secretary.

However it is worked out in each context, there needs to be this threefold strategy: identifying emerging leaders, investing in their development, and entrusting them with significant responsibilities. When we stop to think, this approach is the very strategy that Jesus adopted. The Gospels reveal that at the beginning of his ministry, having chosen the 12 apostles, some of whom at least were young men when they were called, Jesus took the lead and they looked on. Over a three-year period, he spent time with them, inspired, taught and nurtured them. When necessary, he confronted and rebuked them. Then, when he knew the time was right, he gave them opportunities to minister, some of which would be well outside their comfort zone, and for which they felt ill equipped (Luke 10:1–16). But the following verses indicate the sense of joy and fulfilment they experienced as a result of being entrusted with such responsibilities (Luke 10:17–24). After those three years of 'apprenticeship training', it was those disciples to whom he entrusted the task of building his Church.

It is my conviction that one of the reasons many young adults are lost to the Church is that, as well as the Church not being more strategic in investing for the future, they have not been entrusted with the responsibilities of leadership for which they would be more than capable. With appropriate training, oversight and support, it is not uncommon for the planning and delivery of a conference or retreat at Lee Abbey Devon to be in the hands of a 20-year-old host team leader. One such person comments:

> Had you told me when I arrived that I would be trusted with leading the team responsible for a week's programme, I would have laughed. But six months on, I have come to understand that I do have leadership gifts, and with the support of others, it has been a perfect place to develop these skills.

Reflecting on their experience some years on, one former community member summarised their time in Devon in this way:

> It was at Lee Abbey that I was first given the opportunity to test my calling into Christian leadership. This has been very important as I had felt that calling before, but my self-confidence had been battered prior to coming to Lee Abbey, so much so that I wondered if I did after all have leadership gifts. I believe I would not be in my current leadership role, had I not been given opportunities at Lee Abbey.

If that is something of the vision and strategy needed to begin to develop a leadership culture, what kind of qualities do we need to look for in emerging leaders?

My first response to this question is the importance of recognising that leadership has many faces. The image of a leader as an extrovert with a dynamic personality, never happier than when standing in front of large groups of people, is actually a limiting factor when it comes to understanding leadership qualities. It means that significant numbers of people, because they do not fit that particular mould, do not think they have leadership gifts; that if you are a more reflective, introvert personality, somehow you cannot be an effective leader. I have come to understand that different leaders can lead with dramatically different styles. They all have the spiritual gift of leadership, but they express that gift in a rich variety of ways.

This is illustrated by the case of one rather shy, lacking-in-confidence, introvert person who joined the Devon community. Much to her surprise, and that of others, over the two years she was with us she led one of the community's small fellowship groups as well as several host teams, planning and delivering the programme for over 100 guests. Her nature and personality-type remain unchanged, but she is an example of the important discovery that the leadership gift can be expressed in a variety of ways.

Leadership qualities

That said, whatever the leader's personality type, there are certain qualities and areas of competence that need to be present in those taking up leadership responsibilities. At the heart of this must be the person's *character*. Biblically, especially as we read the Pastoral Epistles (1 and 2 Timothy and Titus), it is character that is foremost as a sign that someone can be entrusted with leadership. The reason this is so vital is that a person may be very gifted, and may have that capacity to influence others, but will they use these things wisely and appropriately? While not expecting perfection, it is right to look for a commitment to growth in spiritual maturity. Is there in them also a commitment to the kinds of spiritual disciplines that will enable a growth in holiness? Do I see signs of humility and teachability? In church or community life, an occasional lapse in 'performance' is inevitable, but lapses in character on the part of a leader, as we know, can create problems with far-reaching implications.

If that reflects something of the 'first great commandment', the second vital quality to be discerned in a potential leader reflects the 'second great commandment' – is there evidence of a *love for people*, and appropriate people-skills to match this? By this I mean an awareness of, and sensitivity to, the thoughts and feelings of others; the ability to listen with delight and attentiveness to others, to appreciate and not be threatened by their insights. Whether in church leadership or other leadership responsibilities, this quality also means being willing to learn to relate to a wide range of people, including those carrying wounded histories which may cause them to be demanding and challenging. It means being aware, too, when there might be power issues that have to be faced and dealt with.

Thirdly, the leadership gift expresses itself in people who are willing to *take initiatives* that may well involve risk. Leaders are the kind of people who will ask the question 'Why not?' rather than raise the question 'Why?' The whole Lee Abbey story in a sense exemplifies this. The six men who first saw the house and grounds during the latter years of the Second World War saw the potential for a centre for evangelism and lay training. At the time the property was not for sale, and they had no money, but that did not deter them from seeing the possibilities and committing themselves to prayer over the following years. When it did come on the market in 1945, they signed the contract to buy Lee Abbey, with no money, except a legacy of £6000 that one of the praying group had unexpectedly been left. Over the succeeding years came the vision for what is now the International Students' Club in London, and the development of Household communities working in partnership with inner-city and outer-urban churches.

In recent years in Devon the vision to build a Youth and Outdoor Centre, where young people can come and be stretched physically, educationally and spiritually, represents a further risk-taking initiative. So often the Church is finance- and circumstance-driven, rather than vision-driven, and so does not take risks. What is needed, whether at the level I have just outlined, or in the willingness, for example, to explore new approaches to prayer in worship, is people in whom others have confidence, to take that initiative. Leaders are those who, often themselves in fear and trembling, will make things happen. They themselves have vision and energy and thereby energise and envision others.

A fourth quality to look for is described in some research circles as *'emotional intelligence'*. This is nothing to do with academic qualifications, though we do need leaders who can 'hold their own', especially in the area of apologetics in the postmodern, post-Christian world in which we find ourselves. What I mean is more to do with having an accurate self-awareness, the person knowing their strengths and weaknesses. Do they use time well? Can they prioritise? This area also includes the capacity to process information well, to handle more than one issue at once, to consider different options or courses of action, and generally to make good decisions in which others will have confidence. I would also include in this area an approach to handling conflict that looks for reconciliation rather than letting things go 'underground', or settling for 'peace at any price'.

A commitment to *teamwork*, and not being a 'lone ranger', or worse, a 'prima donna', is the fifth quality we need to see evidence of in an emerging leader. Within the Church, that commitment to teamwork is not simply about learning the importance of working with other people; rather, as the different New Testament metaphors of the Church indicate, it is intended to be about sharing life with one another as people serve together. It is also the recognition that in this changing Church and world, leaders need relationships as well as responsibilities.

In an intentional community setting such as Lee Abbey, Devon, this is at the heart of our three-fold purpose statement: to be God's welcome, to build community and to renew and serve the Church, all under the overall Lee Abbey mission statement of 'communicating Christ through relationships'. However, this understanding of teamwork that we seek to model, albeit imperfectly, put into practice in the local church, in deaneries, dioceses, circuits or districts, could significantly improve the relational 'temperature' of a leadership team anywhere in the world.

Once again, Jesus provides the perfect model of a leader committed to building a team. This is clear all the way through the Gospels, but perhaps nowhere more poignantly than on the eve of his betrayal, when he is in the upper room with his 'team'. He first of all displays the servant-heartedness vital to teamwork and any true understanding of leadership, as he takes a towel and washes the disciples' feet. We then hear these words: 'I have eagerly desired to eat this Passover with you before I suffer' (Luke 22:15 NIV). Following this, he broke the bread and shared the wine, and his instructions for the future were quite specific. The disciples were to 'do this in remembrance of me' (Luke 22:19) – in community. To express it another way, the first time communion was taken, was a team experience. This is why the weekly communion service for the Lee Abbey community (known as 'Corpus', i.e. 'the body') is described in the community promises that people take, as 'the central act of our work and worship'. It is both what sustains that sense of teamwork and what enables it to be a reality. As one community member expressed it: 'I have come to understand that to be a worshipper is not just about sung worship when we come together, it's about lifestyle, how we give our time, what attitude we bring to guests and our fellow community members.'

These five areas do not form an exhaustive list, but I believe they offer a framework in which it is possible to evaluate whether or not someone has leadership gifts. What is also crucial, at this stage in the twenty-first century, is that we recognise that emerging leaders are going to be offering leadership in new ways in a very different kind of Church

from that which many of us are familiar with and have been
operating in. To put it another way, if the current leadership of
the Church has any sense (!), it will listen to 'what the Spirit is
saying to the churches', and put resources and energy into
enabling people to lead new ways of being and doing church,
rather than pushing emerging leaders into what Robert Warren
helpfully calls the 'inherited' mode of being church.

Three key themes

I sense that there are going to be three key themes that will shape
the contours of leadership, and how it will need to express itself
in the coming years. The first is that of connecting with the *search
for spirituality* that so many people are engaged in today. In the
emerging culture, it is not so much the quest for, or defence of, a
'perfect belief system' that is at stake, so much as seeing Christianity as a way of life, or, as a recent retreat weekend at Lee
Abbey was titled, 'exploring Jesus as a journey of spiritual
transformation'. In the climate in which we find ourselves, if
Christianity is not seen to be bearing fruit in a way or rhythm of
life that yields a measure of Christ-likeness, people are rightly
not impressed or interested. The issue is not whether people are
'saved' so much as whether they are being transformed.

In this kind of setting new skills will be demanded of those in
leadership roles. Preaching, for example, both loses and gains
status. Instead of an exercise in transferring information, so that
people have a coherent, well-formed 'worldview', preaching
now and in the future will aim at inspiring transformation. The
gain is that it becomes less about well-reasoned argument, and
more a journey shared by preacher and hearers alike. To change
the imagery, it is allowing God's word to run among people like
water on a field after rain, encouraging fresh green life to spring
up. The preacher becomes less a scholar and more a sage; less a
lecturer, and more a poet and prophet.

All this will require more creativity to be brought to the task of
leadership, especially in the area of worship. Together with

others – and this is where teamwork again is so vital – there needs to be a weaving together of contemporary and ancient threads, so that people, through words, symbol, music, silence and sacrament, can experience transformation, as individuals and as a group.[2]

The second theme is that of *authentic community*. Here, the late Bishop Lesslie Newbigin may prove to be not only one of the most significant theologians of the twentieth century, but also one of the most prophetic voices for emerging and innovative leaders in the twenty-first. In *The Gospel in a Pluralist Society* he comments: 'Jesus did not write a book, but formed a community'.[3] In the same book he goes on to say that 'the greatest hermeneutic of the Gospel, is a community that seeks to live by it'. More recently, the Church of England's *Mission-Shaped Church* Report has expressed this same theme in these words: 'In a missionary church, a community of faith is being formed. It is characterised by welcome and hospitality. Its ethos and style are open to change when new members join.'[4]

Of the thousands of guests who have come to Lee Abbey, Devon, when asked informally, or through evaluation forms, what has been most important, even transformational, about their stay, the highest percentage will say, 'becoming a part of an international community for a few days' or 'sharing the life of the community'. The setting is stunning, the worship, teaching, conversations and other input are important, but it is 'community' that is most significant. Two quotations from guest evaluation forms illustrate this:

> Together with my wife and two friends, I have just returned from my first visit to Lee Abbey. It is hard to find words that express how much the short stay has meant for all of us. We felt a special appreciation for the host teams whose enthusiasm seemed tireless, but realise that the whole community, up front and behind the scenes is what made the experience so special. Please let them know that all they are and do is highly valued.

Each time I come to Lee Abbey, when I leave I say 'that was the best ever', so once again a big 'thank you' to each member of the community, from the bed maker to the preacher! The part that each of the community plays in being God's welcome is just as important. See you in September!

Again, there is nothing new about this, because as we look back down the centuries of Christian history, time after time, God has chosen to renew his Church, especially at times of crisis, through community. The Desert Fathers, the monasteries and orders of Friars in the first 15 centuries of the Church, bear witness to this. The nineteenth-century revival of the religious life in the Anglican Church played its part, as have communities like Taizé and Iona, along with Lee Abbey, Scargill House, the Northumbria Community, the Community of Aidan and Hilda, and other 'lay' communities founded in the twentieth century. (Indeed, it was the challenges of the prophetic report *Towards the Conversion of England*[5] that played a vital part in the vision to found Lee Abbey.)

Emerging leaders will need to be those with a commitment to build authentic community. Sadly, the model that has been evident all too often is one of a church that takes people out of their neighbourhoods and networks, into church activities that isolate them. The vision needs to be of a 'church gathered' in such a way that people are then better equipped to be the 'church dispersed', thus fulfilling Jesus' prayer in John 17, that his followers might not be 'of' the world, but would remain 'in' the world.

This is therefore not a call to seek community as an end in itself, far less an escape from the world, but rather to pursue love as a practice, which yields community as a by-product. In recent years, one of the ways in which Lee Abbey has been seeking to respond to this challenge and to resource leaders has been to offer placements to people at theological or Bible college, as part of their ministerial formation. Similarly, encouraging people to come to Lee Abbey as part of a sabbatical, and in both cases sharing the life and rhythm of the community, seems to give potential and established leaders fresh vision and some tools for that community-building process. Over the years, the context of community has also been one in which many people have found their vocation, whether that is then worked out in ordination, teaching, youth work, the business world, the world of the arts, or a hundred other ways.

If as a result, even a few people in our churches begin to practise a more radical hospitality, or in the words of St Aidan, learn to 'love God and live generously', this might begin to model new ways of life to a frenetic, transient, often broken society. Offering appropriate leadership to enable this will have about it that innovative, risk-taking quality referred to earlier, which will be both more demanding, but also more exciting. Leaders in the emerging culture, I sense, will increasingly resemble the lead seeker in a journey, not being afraid of 'loose ends', or feeling they have to know all the answers. However, they will display a passionate commitment to find a way 'home', and take others on the journey with them.

The third theme which will shape the contours for emerging leaders and the emerging Church is the *missional* one. This appears to be an awkward word – why not simply use the word 'mission'? As I understand it, the concept attempts to integrate everything from racial reconciliation to ecological stewardship, personal evangelism, social action, doing good works, and doing our daily work with goodness. Missional Christianity is trying to say that God is expressing his love for all people through our acts of kindness and service. The invitation is to leave behind a life of accumulation, competitiveness and focus on self, to join the community of God's people in a life of love, fulfilment, blessing and peace. I am finding that many potential and emerging leaders care deeply about both community and context. Mission today is about creating the kind of community that cares for the world in the way that God does.

Mentoring

In the final section of this chapter, I want to focus on the concept of mentoring, which I believe to be of crucial importance in helping to resource emerging leaders. Once more, although there is rightly a strong emphasis on this in many areas of work today, there is nothing new about it, as I will illustrate. (I am deliberately using the word 'mentoring' and not 'coaching' here. Coaching is primarily about skills and competencies, working on a short time-frame. Mentoring takes a longer-term view of the development process, is concerned for the whole person, and has as its primary focus, attitudes, values and vision.)

When I say there is nothing new here, back in the late eighteenth and early nineteenth centuries, when Church life was at a low ebb, if not in crisis, Charles Simeon, Vicar of Holy Trinity Cambridge, for over 50 years, mentored over 1100 young ministers. They caught his vision for a renewed Church, and through his investment of time in them, many parishes across the country were renewed and revived. Those who knew Simeon well acknowledged that he did not seem to be an ideal candidate for being a mentor, so what were his qualities that proved so effective for emerging leaders?

Simeon had a love for his 'protégés' that was genuine and sacrificial. He was concerned to share life as well as information and skills, and as we have seen, that is vital in today's context. Secondly, he had a high, yet realistic view of the call to leadership. He enabled his mentees not to lose sight of its privileges, but also recognised the pressures that come with such responsibility. Simeon encouraged a healthy balance in the leadership role. For him there were three key elements – hard work, study, and exercise. Fourthly, over time, he grew in humility as he recognised that he was on a journey of discovery and had his own limitations. Finally, he offered both formal and informal opportunities for mentoring – weekly sessions on Sundays, and other contacts along the way.

My own practice as a 'training incumbent' in different parish contexts, as well as in my leadership role at Lee Abbey, has been to follow something of this mix of the 'formal' and 'informal' approaches to mentoring. In order to be able to navigate the uncertain currents that lie ahead, emerging leaders will need to have mentors who can create an environment of confidence, that will help to equip, encourage, support, and also give permission to get things wrong, as part of the learning process. De-briefing and ongoing evaluation is also an important part of the mentoring process. Although time-consuming, if we are serious about developing emerging leaders, all this is an investment well worth making, for the present and the future.

Whether a leader is considered as 'emerging' or has 'emerged', either way we have never 'arrived'. Leadership is a commitment to a marathon, not a sprint. Starting may be exciting, but finishing is essential! More important than what we think of ourselves, or what others think of us, is God's perspective. Where anyone ends up on the 'leadership ladder' is unimportant – what we are becoming in Christ-likeness is everything. God's assessment of us will not ultimately be about influence exerted, but did we make it our aim to please him? Was there faithfulness leading to fruitfulness? The 'crown' will not be one of leadership, but 'the crown of righteousness, which the Lord, the righteous judge will award to me on that day' (2 Tim. 4:8).

NOTES

1. See *Fit to Lead* (DLT, 2002) and 'The Vicar's Guide' (Church House Press, 2005).
2. Emma Ineson has written much more about this in Chapter 4, 'Community and Worship'.
3. Lesslie Newbigin, *The Gospel in a Pluralist Society* (SPCK, 1989), p. 227.
4. *Mission-Shaped Church: church planting and fresh expressions of church in a changing context* (London, Church House Publishing, 2004), p. 82.
5. *Towards the Conversion of England* (Westminster, Press and Publications Board of the Church Assembly, 1945).

9

Mat Ineson and
Phil Stone

COMMUNITY AND
YOUNG PEOPLE

Revd Mat Ineson was a Chaplain at Lee Abbey Devon from 2003 to 2006, before which he led the Lee Abbey Youth Camps for seven years. He is now Vicar of St Matthew and St Nathanael, Kingsdown, Bristol.

Revd Phil Stone has led the Lee Abbey Youth Camp since 1993, and has a long association with Lee Abbey. He is now a Team Rector and Area Dean in Brent, London.

Young people have always been a central part of the Lee Abbey movement and its ministry. From its beginnings in Devon there were young people in the community. Currently the average age of community members in Devon is 27 and in London it is 29. Lee Abbey Youth Camps have been operating since 1948 on the field below the house in Devon. The Beacon Youth and Outdoor Centre caters for young people from youth groups and schools and is run by a team of community members, mostly in their twenties. Each of these parts is, and has been, hugely influential in the discipleship and development of many thousands of children and young people. This chapter will draw on some of that experience to encourage other worshipping communities in welcoming, ministering to, investing in and receiving from children and young people.

In Scripture God clearly sees this investment and involvement as part of any worshipping community's life. From the beginnings of the community of Israel, God has urged his people to take time to encourage their younger members in faith and trust in him: 'We will not hide [God's teachings] from our children; we will tell the coming generation the glorious deeds of the Lord, and his might, and the wonders he has done' (Ps. 78:4).[1]

We live today in a very different cultural context, but the principle remains. Part of the task of the Church is to encourage children and young people into discipleship. As we shall see, this leads us to enable young people to discover and exercise their gifts. Our hope is that this chapter will help church communities to take a step in that direction.

Over the past 20 years there has been an explosion of interest in, and new ideas about, how churches can reach and keep young people. Church work with young people has a long history in the UK through Sunday schools, catechism, choirs and the uniformed organisations. As the influence of the Church generally has declined, these strategies have become less effective in many places. There often seems to be a certain amount of guilt-ridden *angst* emanating from churches experiencing a gradual ageing of their worshipping communities and a decline in the number of younger people joining them. However, youth mission and ministry is fast evolving in other arenas. More and more churches are seeking to appoint Youth Workers, recognising the need for this kind of work in their communities. There has been a meteoric rise in large Christian youth events, such as Soul Survivor, and in the number of 'youth churches'. Whilst it is wonderful to see many young people energised in discipleship through these larger gatherings, there still remains the question: 'What next?' What happens to these young people as they return to their smaller communities? What happens as the youth communities they are a part of grow and mature? How can young people be integrated into the worshipping communities of today and be encouraged to be the leaders of tomorrow?

At the outset, it is important to be clear about two things. Firstly, young people are the Church of today as well as the Church of tomorrow. This chapter is not about how we can encourage young people to wait until the future, simply to 'maintain' the Church as it is now. Secondly, we need to remember that whenever we welcome new people, especially young people, into our worshipping community, that community will change and we must be prepared to accept the costs and the joys of that. Any parent will tell you that the introduction of children and young people into a household changes it. It will never be the same again.

A biblical view of young people

One of the biggest mistakes we can make is to assume that young people cannot be used by God. As we read Scripture and reflect on experience, it is clear that God is more interested in gifts than he is in age. Children and young people are, and always have been, part of God's plan. God doesn't wait for people to grow up before he begins to include them and use them in powerful ways. Of course, biblical culture was different. Life expectancy was shorter (unless you were Noah) and there wasn't really the same concept of 'childhood'. But the point still stands. God included very young people in his plans. Joseph received his gift of dreams while he was a youth.[2] Samuel was young when he heard God's call.[3] David fought Goliath when he was a boy[4] (no one else would!). Naaman took advice from his young maid.[5] Josiah became king at the age of eight.[6] The only wisdom Job received from his 'comforters' was from Elihu, who is described as 'young in years'.[7] Jeremiah was told not to use the fact that he was a child as an excuse.[8] Mary was probably a teenager when she gave birth to Jesus.[9] Jesus was talking with the priests at the age of 12.[10] In the early Church it is clear that some of the leaders were young. For example, Timothy was urged not to let people look down on him because of his age.[11] John encourages the young people to be strong.[12]

Youth is looked upon as an asset in the leaders and the prophets of the Bible. The young are often the risk-takers and the challengers. Jesus was well aware of the advantages of youth in terms of faith in God: 'Truly I tell you, whoever does not receive the Kingdom of God as a little child will never enter it.'[13] Age can bring a cynicism that youth is able to cut through with idealistic simplicity.

Another major insight is that the biblical community is always 'all age'. There are no divisions in age or gender or race in the Kingdom of God. There is no doubt that there would have been young people and children meeting together as part of the early Church. In Ephesians 6 there is a section dedicated to encouraging children to obey their parents. Paul would have expected the letter to have been read to the church as a whole and therefore assumed that the children would be present. Lydia's whole household, including children and slaves, were baptised in Acts 16. The young were a valued part of the worshipping culture of the synagogues and the wider society. That norm would have been translated into early Christian worship. We will examine the implications of this in our own culture later in the chapter.

Community as outreach

The vision of the Beacon Youth and Outdoor Centre at Lee Abbey Devon is to 'empower young people by offering an environment where they can stretch themselves mentally, physically and spiritually'. The majority of the guests at the Beacon are not from Christian backgrounds. Many school groups come to the centre to engage in outdoor pursuits and environmental education as part of the National Curriculum. For the duration of their stay they form community; children, young people and adult leaders each with different roles. Much of the work done is 'seed sowing'. Christ is communicated through the stunningly beautiful setting of the centre and through the love shown in relationship between leaders and guests.

The Lee Abbey Youth Camps also operate on community principles. Throughout August at the Devon site there are three camps catering for up to 300 young people between the ages of 13 and 25 and led by a team, many of whom are under 30. Throughout their history the camps have aimed to create a community where it is safe to explore and seek the truth of the Gospel. It is evangelism and discipleship based on relationships between Christian and 'not yet Christian' and between Christian and Christian. Teaching is done didactically during sessions but more is 'learned' through living in, and journeying together through, the truth of the Gospel in community. Leaders are both mentors and role models, teachers and friends.

The Youth Camp and the Beacon demonstrate the benefits of 'doing things' together just for the sake of doing, through 'wasting time' together. This is an integral part of relationship-building with young people. Climbing, playing, creating, listening to music, spending time taking an interest in young people is part of the ongoing welcome. Anyone who has worked with young people knows that respect has to be earned and given. Young people are much more likely to be challenged by another's life if they feel they have a good trusting and honest relationship with that other person. This is true for evangelism and discipling, which both occur best as part of community.

Here again we can see the benefits of an 'all-age' community. Those who respect, accept and take an interest in young people can have an influence on their world-views. The mentoring process comes as a consequence of building significant relationships through 'wasting time' together. Perhaps local church communities would see significant fruit when young people are encouraged and nurtured as part of community. Doing this helps young people to feel accepted for who they are now rather than who we hope they will be. This may not be easy. One of the main difficulties is seeing behind the masks that many young people put on in an attempt to deal with their everyday lives.

Generally speaking, many young people are not readily accepted for who they are by society. They are often seen as 'economic units' in development, or as ill-behaved threats to our personal safety. The real experience of many young people is generally different to this. Those who do not seem open and friendly are very often products of a society that does not value, accept and love them. Young people are not to be kept away until they grow up, but rather welcomed to enable them to grow into loving relationship with others. It's amazing what a casual 'hello' from an older person to a young person walking down a street or past a school gate can signal. It shows young people that they matter.

During the late 1990s a group of young people came to Lee Abbey Camp from an inner-city area. They were overwhelmed by the love and acceptance they received from the Camp community. We won't deny that at first the Camp team was a little apprehensive but after a couple of days of spending time with them, disarming them (literally), accepting and loving them, 'wasting time' with them, they were transformed. They loved Camp and they loved being part of an accepting community. They were loved into life. One of my abiding memories is of one of the older and larger young men sitting with a small candle resting in his huge hands, enjoying a Taizé worship evening! He was being himself with God and that 'being' came from a knowledge of acceptance from the community of which he was a part. Accepting and loving community is healing for young people.

John Robinson was a Lee Abbey Devon community member. During his childhood he was brought up in several foster homes. At 14 he found himself sent to a detention centre. He moved from the Borstal to the streets and on to a psychiatric hospital. He was a scarred and angry young man. Then he met with God. After his dramatic conversion he was lovingly accepted by two families before joining the Lee Abbey community in Devon. He describes the community as a family, a place where he was loved, discipled and disciplined, a place where he grew in faith and in turn discovered his own gifting in working with young people.[14]

John has gone on to work for the Eden Bus project in Manchester. Teams from Eden travel round the inner-city areas, building relationships through playing football with, talking with and accepting young people where they are. When those buses are present, the crime rate drops dramatically. The police are so impressed that they fund some of the work. The teams provide a 'Godly community stop'. Young people experience that somebody cares. God's presence in those teams is beginning to transform the young people.

Boundaries

The acceptance John describes and now models is not a blind acceptance but a loving one. It was tough love. There were boundaries on behaviour. There were difficulties with other individuals, as there always are in community. This kind of welcome is not without risk. Loving acceptance challenges and encourages. So often our communities insist on good behaviour before the welcome. If young people are not shown how to behave, if love has not been modelled, if society at large does not encourage them, then they will not know how to behave. God working through church community can redeem that in any individual, but in order to do that, boundaries must be in place.

When Jesus met the woman caught in adultery[15] he accepted her where she was and for who she was. He loved her. He forgave her. But he also told her to go and sin no more. We must not be afraid of 'tough love', setting boundaries and policing them in a gracious way. At Lee Abbey in Devon there are 'guidelines' for community living rather than 'rules', to do with things such as alcohol and relationships between men and women. The boundaries are clear and it is noticed when they are crossed, but the consequences of that depend on the individual situation. To be a community of grace means acknowledging the wrong and being generous in our treatment of a loved one. Boundaries bring security. They send the message that somebody cares enough to try and protect the life of the community and the individuals that form it. Boundaries are part of acceptance and love of one another.

Churches can model this too. Open youth work is fraught with difficulties but when done well it speaks volumes about God's love for young people. A church in Birmingham that Mat belonged to opened up a youth club in the hall next to the church. There were the inevitable groups of young people milling around on the streets, and there were rules broken and boundaries crossed but there were also seeds sown. Some of those young people are now working in Christian community projects in Birmingham. Being welcoming and accepting is risky. It changes those doing the welcoming as well as those being welcomed.

Belonging

Each of us has a need to belong. In the Genesis creation account only one thing is not good. It is not good for the man to be alone.[16] Adam is in the perfection of the Garden of Eden, intimately related to God – and he is lonely! We were created to be in community, to belong to others.

What do we need to feel that we belong? We know we belong when we feel accepted, when we are given roles in communities, when we become known, when we have spent time with others, when we feel that our presence can influence the community in which we live. Belonging is a two-way process – how we are welcomed, accepted and loved, and how seriously we are taken.

There are many myths about what 'belonging' means. Joseph Myers identifies five.[17] He argues that belonging is not about spending more time together, or about promising more commitment or about common purpose or personality or small groups. Belonging in our current context is, perhaps unsurprisingly, about relationships and mutual experience. It happens when 'you identify with another entity',[18] and it happens on many levels.

In the past people would have been happy to belong to an institution or would have allied themselves to a set of beliefs, which they 'belonged to'. But today's young people live in a cultural context where belonging is about sharing experience. Understanding is not a necessary precursor. It is about whether or not it 'feels' right. In the light of this, how can we encourage belonging in young people in our churches? One of the primary ways is by making connections, by taking time to welcome, and by loving.

The Beacon Youth Centre recently hosted a group of young people from an inner-city area. They were welcomed and hosted in the usual way. But as the week went on it became clear that they struggled to behave in a way that enabled any of the planned activities to go ahead. They were unruly and uncooperative. The normal week's activities didn't work. Archery was, frankly, just too dangerous and had to be abandoned. But throughout the weekend discipline was kept tight and loving. It was described as a 'loving battle'. On the final morning some of the Beacon team shared their stories and sang for the group. All of the young people listened in respectful silence. God touched their lives through the love (sometimes tough love) shown by the team. And through the team's sharing the young people were drawn into the community. They belonged through loving association.

When Jesus was asked, 'Who is my neighbour?' he answered with the parable of the good Samaritan, which showed that your neighbour is the next person you meet who needs your love.[19] The next person we meet is loved by God and therefore belongs in the Church.

Lee Abbey's Knowle West Household community is on an outer estate in Bristol. Local young people know that they are welcome at the house, whether that's for a chat or to have their bikes fixed. The young people who visit are not large in number but they do feel valued, accepted and cared for because the leaders of the Household take time with them. In very practical ways, they are being their neighbours.

Belonging helps form identity

During adolescence a young person's biggest question is 'Who am I?' This is not a question that can be answered in isolation, because we are created to be in community. The formation of our identity is to be discovered in our relationships with others. This is particularly true of young people.[20] Whilst home and family are important for most young people, identity cannot be formed here alone. At this stage of life the community that they belong to can have an enormous effect on who they become.

Part of the discovery of 'Who am I?' requires a natural separation from my family. The home can be vitally important as a foundation and a base from which to learn, but as young people mature, they seek role models outside the home in order to help them define themselves. These can be peers and also mentors. Where we belong in our teenage years can significantly affect the way we see ourselves. It is part of the formation of our identity. Church communities can play a significant role in this process.

One of the major benefits of 'all-age' community is the potential for those who are older to 'role model' good, Christ-focused relationships. Many young people come into community at Lee Abbey Devon and London with wounded histories. Some need specific healing ministry and counselling but a great deal of healing happens through normal loving relationships. One recent community member expressed this when she said that her relationships with Christian men in the community had been very healing for her. They had enabled her to lay aside some of the more harmful relationships with men that she had experienced in the past. At Lee Abbey she said she felt affirmed as a woman and loved for who she was rather than what she looked like. Belonging is enabling her to become herself and to find her identity.

This process of discovering self often comes through pain as well as through loving and being loved. We often learn more about ourselves from those we find difficult than from those who it is easy to love. One of the great lessons that community teaches is how to engage with others in conflict and how to deal with the fallout from that conflict. Forgiveness is part and parcel of loving. Leaders and mentors in communities need to take time to help young people through conflict, enabling the healthy creativity of conflict to inform and nourish their sense of belonging. This can be done through peer-group cells or simply through mentoring friendship.

One of the most moving moments that Mat has experienced at Lee Abbey Devon was a public confession of sin involving a young person from the community. The young man courageously stood before the whole community and expressed his sorrow for his actions. Through this we all learnt the effect of an individual's sin on a community. Rather than deepening the wound, the public confession increased the love shown to the young man involved, enabling him to feel forgiven and strengthened by the community.

Young people belonging changes the community

When people are welcomed, they change the community into which they come. We feel this very strongly at Lee Abbey Devon. Every year we have a 70 per cent turnover of community members. Those of us privileged to stay in the community for longer observe that each year is different. In fact, whenever someone leaves or joins, the community changes. Community is made up of individuals called by God to belong together. When the individuals change, the community also changes.

This is true for church communities too. When new people, particularly young people, join a church and are welcomed, things will change. Belonging requires that the community adjusts to receive the new person, perhaps sacrificing some of its behaviours. It may also require that the new person adjusts. We have heard many bemoan the lack of young people in their church communities. But when it is suggested that worship patterns (for example) might need to change in order to attract and keep young people, this idea is met with horror. We cannot expect young people to come and then maintain the way that we want things to be. We have to be willing to learn from their expression of worship in the same way that we hope they may learn something of God from ours.

Community as a safe place to explore and nurture faith

As Camp leaders, on occasion we have had people questioning whether Lee Abbey Camp is teaching Christianity 'properly' because we allow people to explore issues of faith for themselves within the confines of a safe community, rather than laying it out in a didactic way. We believe this approach resonates more readily with the critical nature of young people. Young people are critical, that's how they learn, that's how they are taught to learn in school. As they mature, the questions become increasingly critical. This is a natural part of growing up. They will question faith and we need to be willing to listen and to enable them to find the answers.

One of the most challenging characteristics about children and young people is their ability to ask questions. In Luke 2 the boy Jesus is in the temple. He's been left by accident and his parents are searching for him. They find him in the temple listening to the teachers and asking them questions. Asking questions enables understanding. But it also requires a safe, loving community within which to ask and explore.

A Bible verse that sums up the philosophy of Lee Abbey Youth Camp is Psalm 18:19: 'He has brought me out into a spacious place; he has rescued me because he delighted in me.' Camp is a 'spacious place' both physically and spiritually. That spaciousness is liberating for many. Becoming part of a loving community brings freedom; hearts are opened to love, minds are renewed, and lives are changed by the love of Christ. Jesus' words, 'if the Son shall set you free – you shall be free indeed'[21] are realised by many. There is a spiritual law beautifully put in the story of the Velveteen Rabbit[22] – 'the more you are loved the more real you become'. Camp models the reality of that phrase.

In terms of Christian faith, spaciousness does not mean 'anything goes'. That would be overwhelming. But the boundaries are not made explicit. They are defined and communicated through the lives of the believing community rather than written laws. It is a place of grace rather than law, a fellowship not a pharisaic institution. Such 'spaciousness' is risky because to encourage exploration rather than direction removes control. And here's the crux of the matter: we all have to learn to own our faith. This means working through things for ourselves, growing up from inherited faith to a living faith that works for me now.

Young people come to faith and grow in faith through discovery. Through our experience as teachers of young people we have found that didactic styles of teaching are valuable, but the fruits of discovery and exploration are much longer lasting. Young people like to question and explore everything as part of growing up. Churches should not be afraid of giving them that freedom, of allowing them to question and seek, to try out new ideas, to test out why those of us who are older have made the decisions we have made about our lives. Are we as church willing to be questioned by the young people that we have nurtured or encouraged, and are we willing to be changed as part of that dialogue?

We wonder if as church we are sometimes overly concerned with keeping our young people 'on the straight and narrow'. Jesus often teaches in a positive way by encouraging his disciples to do as he does. He asks them to follow and discover the truth that will set them free. He doesn't walk behind them shouting at them when they deviate.

Mentoring

The key to this exploration is the formation of community relationships between young people and older people, or mentors.
Whilst Mat was growing up he had an older friend whom he
would go to and ask questions of. That relationship was really
important in Mat's faith journey, in understanding what faith
meant to his friend and why he believed it. It allowed for the
classic questions of sex, suffering and creation to be explored in
the context of a safe community, as well as enabling discipleship
of a young man growing up in a difficult world.

A wonderful biblical example of mentoring is the relationship
between Eli and Samuel. There was gentleness in the conversation between them as Samuel was being called.[23] Although Eli
was near the end of his life, he nurtured and cherished Samuel.
Eli eventually realised that the Lord was speaking to Samuel,
and he instructed him in how to listen and respond. The message
was hard for Eli to hear,[24] for God was doing something new
which would make ears 'tingle', and it was going to happen
through the young Samuel. This relationship was beautiful and
loving. Without Eli's wisdom the young Samuel would not have
discerned God's voice for him.

Churches can play an important role in encouraging mentoring alongside other relationships with peers, youth groups,
parents and the wider church family. Incidentally, often the
people who are 'good' at listening and talking with young
people are those of 'grandparent' age. In his book *Growing
Community*, Danny Brierley talks about forming small
agenda-less mentoring cell groups that meet and talk and
listen and share. These groups are both missionary in the sense
that they are open, and mentoring in the sense that, if they are
led well, they enable people to discuss how their relationship
with Christ affects the way they live. The technology of the age
can be usefully used to communicate and encourage discipleship in young people. Mat used to send his youth group
encouraging scriptures by mobile text messaging during exam

time. Bible notes can now be obtained by email.[25] Message boards and blogs can also be used.

There are obviously issues of child protection here and any mentoring relationships must be accountable and safe for all concerned. However, it would be a shame if we let fear over such matters inhibit good and healthy relationships across age groups.

Christianity is radical

Young people love all things 'radical'. Christianity *is* radical. So why don't young people love Christianity? Are we guilty of watering the Gospel down to personal salvation and neglecting the social and justice aspects? What kind of Gospel do we present? In her brilliant book *Wild Gospel*[26] Alison Morgan argues that we have tamed the wildness of the Gospel of Christ. We have tamed the person of Jesus to one who is meek and mild. On reading the Gospel accounts, we see a Jesus who was radical, a Jesus who was outspoken about social injustice and religious oppression, a Jesus who was not afraid to challenge, a Jesus who offered freedom and a new way to live. Where is the communication of the 'Wild Gospel'? Where do we encourage our young people in their idealism and help them to challenge the presuppositions and worldviews that they absorb from the outside world, exploring with them what the world says about issues and then enabling them to apply their critical thinking to the underlying assumptions?

At the Youth Camp and the Beacon the leaders run workshops on subjects ranging from world trade and global warming to pornography, bio-ethics, sexuality, materialism and Harry Potter. Young people are encouraged at school to think about and study these things. They love to discuss them and reflect theologically about them. There are many resources available to help in these discussions.[27]

Young people can be idealistic. Often they abhor injustice, as the popularity amongst the young of the 'Make Poverty History' campaign showed. We shouldn't be afraid of engaging with young people in these topics, encouraging them to take action and supporting them in it, thereby showing them that Christianity is a faith of action as well as belief, and encouraging them to take their place within the community. Many young people are highly perceptive. They love to discuss, argue and debate. Yet so much of our youth work seems to be about keeping young people safe from the 'dark world' rather than encouraging them to challenge and question the world in which they live from the basis of biblical truth.

In the story of Job, many 'wise' comforters come to listen and advise, but the one who is closest to God is young Elihu. In his reply to Job (chapters 32—37) Elihu speaks of God's justice, goodness and majesty and condemns self-righteousness. The last few verses of chapter 32 describe a young man who cannot contain himself any longer; he must speak. As well as teaching and encouraging young people in their faith through our communities, we need to remember to listen for God speaking through them.

Young people and worship

There is a common misconception that young people only like a particular style of worship. However, in our experience, young people are as varied in their preferences as everyone else. Many young people appreciate a sense of the mystical, they like space and silence and candles and incense, they like drums and guitars. The key is not so much the content but the context. The 'spaciousness' principle applies here as it does in discipleship. The aim of worship is to draw people into a space where they can meet with God and God with them. A variety of tools can be used, sometimes simultaneously. Art, activity, music to listen to, music to take part in, symbols, teaching, small-group work, visual aids and technology and much more can be utilised to create an environment in which young people can corporately worship, experiencing the presence of God. Labyrinths and prayer stations can be very effective in engaging with the spirituality of many young people, because they allow freedom of expression and are participative.

Worship on the Lee Abbey Camp field draws on a broad spectrum of influences, from Taizé to Vineyard to traditional Catholic. The young people appreciate it because it is authentic to the worshipping community created for those weeks, because they have a relationship with those who are leading and planning it and because they are involved. They know they belong to the community that is worshipping and they are participants, not observers.

About a year ago, one of the campers was so challenged by a leader about his church attendance that he began to cycle to a small rural church from his home every Sunday. He was (thankfully) welcomed and came to belong to that fellowship. He still attends, even though the worship style is not what you would expect him to take part in. He belongs and therefore he worships. He is becoming involved in the life of the church. It is possible.

Participation is important. By this we don't mean that young people have to lead every aspect of worship. Nor do we mean that young people need to be given 'jobs to do'. We mean that there must be opportunities for young people to actively engage with the worship. This is partly about belonging but also about ownership. Many churches have teams that plan worship and some young people would value being part of these teams. Can young people be involved in planning, leading and shaping our worship? Can all ages take active part through discussion, through activities, through music or technology? Can young people see other young people involved? There is a place for children's and young people's groups, but if we expect young people to graduate to 'adult' styles of worship, then we must be inclusive and accessible to all, at least some of the time. If we can model worship whereby all ages are involved, where all ages praise together, pray together, learn together and participate together, then that speaks volumes about the importance of young people in our worshipping communities. This may require us to modify our preferred worship style.

We are very aware that Lee Abbey has many more resources at its disposal than the average church. But little things can make a difference. Using stones as a representation of sin and laying them at the front, or at a cross; writing prayers on Post-it notes and offering them together on a sheet of paper; dramatised readings, and group discussions and activities can all be done with few resources but with a little imagination.[28]

Recently Phil's church youth group led the Mothering Sunday service; every aspect of the service was constructed by the young people. The immediate outcome has been the forming of a youth band which will now be developed to lead worship at the main Sunday service once a month. Also a new youth leader has been identified who has a gift in worship leading. Involving young people in services appropriately is helping to give a multi-generational aspect to the main service. This is itself a sign of the Kingdom and has a prophetic message for the rest of the community.

Godly potential

We saw at the beginning of the chapter that God uses young people in his Church. Young people have gifts to be used now as well as nurtured for the future. One of the great privileges of pastoring Camp teams and communities is seeing God develop and grow gifts in individuals that blossom into fruit for the Kingdom. There are many people around the world today who are using gifts discovered and nurtured within the Lee Abbey movement: leadership gifts, creative gifts, pastoral gifts, gifts of intercession and many others. Many of these gifts come to light by making the space for them to blossom.

Young people often don't have the confidence to believe they are gifted or indeed to use their gifts and skills. It may be that a gift is discerned by a peer or mentor. Our task as churches is to encourage and nurture them. Leaders need to be prepared to take risks in allowing young people to test their raw gifting. Mistakes will be made and sometimes the leader *could* do it better. But if God has given a gift, then it is our responsibility to train, mentor and encourage young people in their gifts for the good of the Church.

Young people and the local church

We are very aware that these ideas sound good but in reality they are often hard to live out. They take energy, resources and patience. Enabling young people to be a part of our communities involves risks. Taking on the ethos of spaciousness often takes a lot of imagination, vision, and risk. It can be expensive in time and money. There may be disappointments as well as encouragements. But what we hope we have encouraged is a mindset that views young people as valued members of church communities now and treats them as such. That may require change.

The attitude of the church community needs to move from the cynical view wrought by disappointment. We've heard church leaders joke that the best way to lose young people from your church is to confirm them. This probably says something about the church rather than the teenager!

The key is in creating an attitude within church leadership and whole church communities that values the creative challenge of young people and allows them a spacious plateau on which to explore Christian faith, to learn to own and experience it for themselves. This involves investing in relationships that allow nurturing and mentoring to occur so that faith can be modelled and passed on. It involves letting go and allowing fresh expressions of faith within the church community. It involves welcoming young people and making a long-term investment in them. It involves love of the person as they are, not moulding them to suit our expectations. It involves allowing mistakes to be made and forgiving and learning from them. Above all, it involves being the body of Christ together – younger and older.

NOTES

1. See also Deut. 6.
2. Gen. 37:2.
3. 1 Sam. 3.
4. 1 Sam. 17.
5. 2 Kings 5:2–4.
6. 2 Chr. 34:1.
7. Job 32:6.
8. Jer. 1:6–7.
9. Luke 1:26ff.
10. Luke 2:46–7.
11. 1 Tim. 4:12.
12. 1 John 2:13–14.
13. Luke 18:17.
14. John Robinson (with Brenda Sloggett), *Nobody's Child* (Monarch, 2003).
15. John 8:1–11.
16. Gen. 2:18.
17. Taken from Joseph R. Myers, *The Search to Belong* (Zondervan, 2003).
18. Ibid., p. 25.
19. Luke 10:25–37.
20. See Erik Erikson's eight stages of human development at www.psychology. about.com/library
21. John 8:36.
22. Margery Williams, *The Velveteen Rabbit* (Egmont Books, 2004).
23. 1 Sam. 3.
24. 1 Sam. 3:11.
25. For example, www.word-on-the-web.co.uk
26. Alison Morgan, *Wild Gospel* (Monarch, 2004).
27. See the work of Nick Pollard of the Damaris Trust (www.damaris.org), which has pioneered work encouraging young people to critically assess their worldviews and assumptions. See also the work of the London Institute of Contemporary Christianity (www.licc.org.uk).
28. Some excellent resources for participative worship are produced by CPAS, Scripture Union and others.

10
Alan Smith

COMMUNITY AND
MISSION

Rt Revd Alan Smith was a Chaplain at Lee Abbey Devon from 1984 to 1989. He was a member of the Lee Abbey Council for many years and was also Chair of the Lee Abbey Household Communities. He has been Bishop of Shrewsbury since 2002.

What is mission?

Christians have used the word 'mission' in different ways during the past two thousand years. Until the sixteenth century it was only used to describe the doctrine of the Trinity: 'the sending of the Son by the Father and of the Holy Spirit by the Father and the Son'.[1] Mission was understood in terms of who God is (one God in three persons) and what God does (engaging with the world that he has created). However, in the sixteenth century a new use of the word emerged. As Bosch observed, 'The Jesuits were the first to use it [the word 'mission'] in terms of the spread of the Christian faith among people (including Protestants) who were

not members of the Catholic Church'.[2] It is in the sense of
Christians spreading the faith that most people tend to use the
word today, although most churches and most Christians still
think that mission is something that usually happens elsewhere,
far away from home. Living in Christendom, we send missionaries to other parts of the world. We pray for them and give
money to support them in their humanitarian work and Christian witness, but this is the extent of our involvement. At home
the only way that we have used the word 'mission' was to speak
of 'mission churches' (which usually meant those which were
not yet strong enough to be churches in their own right), and
occasionally a parish would hold 'a mission' trying to make
contact with people in the area, in the hope that they would start
to come to church.

In recent decades there has been both a re-emphasis on the
original understanding of the word 'mission' and a development
in its use. There has been a reaffirmation that mission is rooted in
who God is (in his 'being' as Trinity) and what he does. It is now
acknowledged by all the major Christian denominations that
mission describes the way in which God is involved in the
world, reconciling the whole of creation to himself.[3] Second, to
be the Church of Jesus Christ is to be inextricably involved in
mission. Indeed, you cannot be a Christian in the fullest sense of
the word unless you are caught up in God's work.[4] In the
theology of the Second Vatican Council, the Church does not
have missions, it *is* mission; it is sent by God into the world as the
sacrament of his presence. Third, one aspect of mission is
evangelism, which Bosch[5] describes as:

> the proclamation of salvation in Christ to those who do not
> believe in him, calling them to repentance and conversion,
> announcing forgiveness of sin, and inviting them to become
> living members of Christ's earthly community and to begin
> a life of service to others in the power of the Holy Spirit.

Although the Acts of the Apostles contains a number of
descriptions of the Church engaged in mission and evangelism,

it is noteworthy that the New Testament contains comparatively
few injunctions to engage in it. There are, of course, the com-
mands to 'love one another' and 'to love one's neighbour'. There
are also the well-known commissions at the end of Mark's
Gospel ('Go into all the world and proclaim the good news to the
whole creation', Mark 16:15) and Matthew's Gospel ('Go and
make disciples of all the nations', Matt. 28:19). There is Paul's
command to Timothy to 'proclaim the message; be persistent
whether the time is favourable or unfavourable' (2 Tim. 4:2), and
Peter's words that we should 'always be ready to make your
defence to anyone who demands from you an account of the
hope that is in you' (1 Pet. 3:15). But why are there so few such
exhortations? Part of the reason is that the first Christians were
so radical in sharing their lives that mission and evangelism
were simply taken for granted. In other words, mission arose out
their 'being' (that is, living counter-culturally in a new community) as well as their 'doing'.

The two aspects of mission and evangelism ('being' and
'doing') are found, intimately linked, in the description of the
early Church in Acts 2:

> They [the believers] devoted themselves to the apostles'
> teaching and fellowship, to the breaking of bread and the
> prayers. Awe came upon everyone, because many wonders
> and signs were being done by the apostles. All who
> believed were together and had all things in common; they
> would sell their possessions and goods and distribute the
> proceeds to all, as any had need. Day by day, as they spent
> much time together in the temple, they broke bread at
> home and ate their food with glad and generous hearts,
> praising God and having the goodwill of all the people.
> And day by day the Lord added to their number those who
> were being saved (verses 42–47).

This radical, counter-cultural living was a feature of the Christian Church in the early centuries. We know that around AD 400

the church in Antioch supported 3000 virgins and widows and the church in Constantinople financed the care of 50,000 poor.[6] It is not surprising that the pagan world was puzzled, annoyed and even threatened by such extraordinary altruism. Nor is it surprising that such practical faith was immensely attractive and the Church grew quickly.

The charism of Lee Abbey: a community or a mission movement?

Trawling through the Lee Abbey archives reveals a tension that has existed since the very beginning of the movement in the 1940s. For some the fundamental calling (or 'charism') of Lee Abbey was to be a home missionary movement. Certainly Roger de Pemberton's vision was for evangelism and training in evangelism, and he planned to employ a permanent pastoral staff to run Lee Abbey. It was only during the early months of Lee Abbey that the newly arrived Christians began to work out what it meant to live together. They had to discover what would be an appropriate pattern of daily prayer and worship. It was at a very early stage that some people began to see that the concept of community was not incidental to Lee Abbey but was a fundamental part of what God was bringing into being.

The tension in Lee Abbey between being primarily a mission movement (focused outwards on the world) or primarily a community (focused on its members) has never been finally resolved and at least some of us feel that this is providential. If Lee Abbey were simply a group of individual missionaries and evangelists, it would be all too easy to lose touch with the challenges of living out the Gospel. If the whole emphasis were on a common life, it would be very easy for Lee Abbey to become self-absorbed, with little concern for the spreading of the faith and the needs of the world.

During the 1990s there were a number of meetings at which this tension was explored. Out of these times of prayer, Bible study and discussion came the idea of 'Sharing Christ through

Relationships', which has come to sum up how the communities hold together the two different emphases of Lee Abbey and its work.

Living creatively with this tension of 'being and doing', of 'living the Gospel and proclaiming it', is also an important task for the leader of every local church. It is possible for a congregation to become so outwardly focused on evangelism that it neglects its own spiritual life and relationships, or on the other hand to become so self-absorbed that there is nothing distinctive about its corporate life. St Basil the Great's question to hermits in the fourth century is applicable to every Christian community: 'Whose feet do you wash?' The twofold task for a Christian leader is to build up a strong sense of commitment and belonging within the Christian community at the same time as focusing the prayer and energy of its members outwards into the service of the wider community.

Lee Abbey and mission today

Over the past six decades the constituent parts of Lee Abbey have expressed their mission and evangelism in a variety of ways. However, a number of common threads have been fairly constant.

Vibrant personal faith

First, the parts of the movement have all shared the conviction that the only basis of mission and evangelism is a *vibrant personal faith*. In other words, sharing the Gospel is not just sharing a message. It is sharing what we have already received from God. Indeed, it has been argued that mission and evangelism are the overflow of our spiritual encounters and journeys. At the heart of the Lee Abbey movement is the biblical invitation that people need to surrender their lives to God and have a personal experience of his love and forgiveness.[7] Only then are they likely to want to go out to others in costly service and witness. Four of the Community Promises reflect this fundamental need to nurture one's spiritual life:

- Do you affirm before the Community your personal faith in Christ and your desire through prayer, study and service to seek a deep and mature faith?
- Do you understand by this that your mind, your time, your talents, your possessions and all your relationships are to be increasingly surrendered to Christ as Lord?
- Have you accepted the discipline of regular private recollection through Bible reading and daily prayer?
- Do you intend to make the weekly Corporate Communion the central act of your work and worship?

It is significant that where there is growth in the Church today, it is often associated with the renewing of personal faith, such as that engendered by the Charismatic movement, pilgrimages to holy places, Cursillo, Sant' Egidio, Taizé or the Focolare movement. Unless we spend time in the presence of God, there will be no motivation or even energy to share the faith. This is, perhaps, one of the biggest challenges facing the Church today. As Pope Paul VI put it:

> The Church is an evangelizer but she begins by being evangelized herself. She is a community of believers, the community of hope, loved and communicated ... She always needs to be called afresh by him and reunited. In brief, this means that she has a constant need of being evangelized. She wishes to retain freshness, vigour and strength in order to proclaim the gospel.[8]

This emphasis on personal faith and renewal has been a challenge to church leaders, which is why many of them have brought groups to stay at Lee Abbey and have also been inspired to work and pray for the renewing of individual Christians in their own churches and parishes. Many clergy know how easy it is for a congregation to lapse into doing religious or churchy things (such as the annual fete) and lose sight of the spirituality which is at the heart of the faith.

It is interesting that people often experience renewal when they are away from home, which is why for hundreds of years Christians have made pilgrimages. The combination of being taken out of the regular routine of daily life and being thrown together with a group of strangers who are also seeking God is a powerful mix.[9] However, rightly used in a way which respects people's integrity and stands alongside them in their searching for a deeper knowledge of God, it can be a time of Christian recommitment and growth. This was the insight behind the house-parties, conferences, retreats and holiday weeks in Devon (including the summer camps) and the life at the Lee Abbey International Students' Club. Thousands of people have en-countered God in some new way whilst staying at Lee Abbey and have returned home with a fresh determination to live for Christ. Any church leader is well advised to take people out of their normal situations and to provide space for them to meet with God. Parish weekends, pilgrimages, quiet days and retreats are an integral part of most flourishing churches.

Something to be shared

Second, the Lee Abbey movement has believed that the good news of Jesus Christ is *something to be shared* and that we should *expect* people to commit their lives to God. For many years the standard programme at the holiday weeks in Devon included a series of epilogues, leading up to Thursday evening, which was the time when a particular challenge was put to the guests to make a Christian commitment. For those who wished to respond, they were invited to make their way to the chapel to pray, either by themselves or with someone else. Over the dec-ades hundreds of people have chosen to respond, and are happy to point to this time as a turning-point in their lives. In recent years prayer and the laying on of hands (sometimes with

anointing) has also been offered and this has also been extremely
important for many of the guests.

Many churches are reticent or embarrassed about asking
people to 'make a commitment to Christ'. There are often good
reasons for this. We do not want to pressurise people and we run
away from any suggestion of proselytising. Perhaps one of the
reasons why the Alpha course has had an impact is that it has
made such an opportunity an integral part of the course. In more
traditional settings, such as the Roman Catholic Rite of Initiation
(RCIA), people are invited to offer themselves to God in a
liturgical setting of baptism (and sometimes confirmation) on
Easter Eve. Many Anglicans have also drawn on insights from
the catechumenate,[10] and a corporate act of re-commitment is
often part of confirmation services today. It is a useful task for
leaders of churches to reflect on the opportunities that are
offered for people to commit (or re-commit) their lives to God.
Some years ago I was involved in the life of a church which used
each January as a time of reflection and commitment. For two or
three weeks sermons and house groups focused on God's call
and invitation. Then towards the end of the month (and using
material from the Methodist Covenant Service) all members of
the congregation were invited to renew their faith and discipleship, and the church leaders (both ordained and a considerable
number of lay leaders) were prayed for with the laying on of
hands. There was also an invitation for any who did not consider
themselves to be Christians to 'offer as much as they knew of
themselves to as much as they knew of God'. This annual process gave the church's year an added dynamism. We knew that
we were moving forward together and it highlighted the need
for all of us to continue growing in faith and obedience.

The priority of personal witness has also been crucial in other
parts of the movement, such as the summer camps, where most
of the sessions for the young people include personal testimony
from members of the camp team. The Lee Abbey International
Students' Club has given a high priority to personal witness,
although living alongside people over a longer period has

created a slightly different dynamic. Community members often comment that the students are very aware of any inconsistencies between witnessing in word and in deed and are not slow in pointing it out. For the London community, the witnessing often has to be a far more subtle thing. However, one is reminded of the words of Leo the Great writing about the martyrdom of St Laurence: 'Eloquence may enable intercession, reasoning may succeed in persuading; but in the end examples are always more powerful than words, and teaching communicates better through practice than precept.'

Lee Abbey's stress on personal evangelism, as one aspect of mission, has been a constant reminder to the wider Church that it is vitally important that the faith is handed on to the next generation.

Living it out in our daily lives

Third, there has always been an emphasis on not just preaching the Gospel but also on *living it out in our daily lives*. For the vast majority of community members a typical day in one of the communities is not very exciting. It is likely to involve cleaning bedrooms, preparing food, or working in an office. For those in the Household communities it may mean having an ordinary job in the locality or working with some voluntary organisation. Some people balk at this or are disappointed. However, it is interesting to reflect that in the Rule of St Benedict, which became the standard work for all Christian community living for over a thousand years, he instructs the abbot to ensure that would-be members of his community not only seek God but, as he puts it, 'are zealous for humiliations'. Benedict is here using a technical word designating the tasks that a slave had to do in the latter days of the Roman Empire. In other words, what St Benedict was saying was that for a Christian community to function well, it needed to have its spiritual heart focused not only on the worship of God but also on a shared commitment to undertake the boring and mundane jobs without which any household disintegrates.

This quiet witnessing through acts of service is fundamental to the mission of the Church. Some years ago I was privileged to visit the Community of Sant' Egidio in Rome. The community was founded in 1968 by Andrea Riccardi, a young man who gathered together some students in order to live out the teaching of the Gospels. Soon God led them to work in the slums on the edge of Rome, running afternoon schools (*Scuola Popolare*). Their life focuses on three main areas: prayer (by which they mean joining together to listen to the Scriptures and to offer themselves to God and to others), communicating the good news of Jesus Christ (by living and sharing the Gospel) and friendship with the poor. Today there are more than 30,000 members living in more than 30 countries. Their life is a powerful witness of the love of God, lived out in costly service.

Lay ministry

Fourth, Lee Abbey has always stressed the importance of *lay ministry* and lay witness. Although this is a biblical concept, in the 1940s, when Lee Abbey was founded, many clergy and laity thought that this was a radical and even dangerous idea. These were still the days when in the Anglican Church the parish priest led every part of public worship and lay people were not even allowed to read or lead prayers in church.

At the opening of Lee Abbey in June 1946 Cuthbert Bardsley spoke of two essential things:

> the creation of confessed and confessing Christians, men and women whose hearts the Lord has touched, who have working experience of the forgiveness and love of Jesus Christ ... and who are able intelligently to introduce other people to the saving grace of Christ.

The second need was to have not merely lone-wolf Christians, but teams; 'an atom force of spiritual energy that nothing can resist'.[11]

Nowadays most churches are familiar with the idea of every-member ministry and many have authorised lay teams. Much of this has come about through movements like Lee Abbey and has become mainstream in most denominations. In the Church of England it received a fresh emphasis through the Tiller Report, published in 1983.[12] At the time many people felt that the report was soon buried and forgotten. However, many of the ideas have gradually received acceptance and, in a variety of different ways, have been implemented.

The need to equip lay people has been undertaken in many ways. All of the Lee Abbey communities believe that an important part of their work is to train community members for lifelong, and in most cases, lay ministry. Therefore all members attend a training course when they join a community and are also able to undertake further study during their time there. In the Devon community another strand has been the series of conferences, mainly held between September and June, which offer training for guests and incidentally for those community members who are on the host team that week. A further aspect of lay ministry has been the mission teams, which were started in the 1940s. There have been many different sorts of mission teams over the years, often with a different emphasis depending upon the views and convictions of the community leaders at that time. Typically, mission teams have been drawn from all the different communities and in some cases have included Lee Abbey Friends of Jesus. More recently there has been a fresh emphasis on resourcing the lay and ordained leaders of local churches in Devon, with a series of day conferences held at Lee Abbey and other local venues.

The Lee Abbey Friends of Jesus were formed in 1947. The Friends were admitted at the end of each house-party and committed themselves to be 'prepared to work through prayer and witness for the conversion of others' and 'to pray regularly for the renewal of the Church, for the work of Lee Abbey and for the other Friends'. Groups of Lee Abbey Friends meet around the country on a regular basis, not as an alternative to their local church, but in order to pray for mission and evangelism locally, and to support the work of the different aspects of the Lee Abbey movement.

Lay ministry and lay witness is a fundamental part of the work of the local church today. Most churches are glad to harness the energies and expertise of a wide range of people from the congregation. However, where the Church has much to learn is in the area of *discerning* people's gifts and in offering proper *training*. All too often the biblical concept of every-member ministry has become confused and it is presumed that it means that anybody can have a go at any aspect of ministry. We all accept that it would be nonsense to expect each member of the congregation to take their turn on the organ stool, so why do we presume that anyone can read the Scriptures, lead prayers, visit the sick or lead a homegroup? An essential part of leadership is to identify people's gifts and then offer them appropriate training. On a regular basis in Devon there are discipleship training courses for community members which are attempts to enable people to grow in faith and equip them for whole-life discipleship.

On a visit to an Episcopal church in the United States of America some time ago I was impressed with the way that members of the congregation were offered help and training. It was not just the children who attended Sunday school. After the morning service there were courses for the adults, lasting for about one and a half hours each week. These ran for different lengths of time, some for just a few weeks, others over a whole year. A wide variety of topics were offered during the year, including foundation courses on the Old Testament and the New Testament, Bible study, pastoral skills (such as counselling, visiting and listening), contemplative prayer, outreach and 'faith and work'. This experience made me realise that most churches in Britain have hardly begun to take lay formation and training seriously.

Not limited to one style

A fifth aspect of Lee Abbey's mission has been the insistence that
the movement should *not be limited to one style of churchmanship or
one denomination.* It was Roger de Pemberton, an Evangelical,
who was very keen that Jack Winslow, an Anglo-Catholic,
should join the community. Later a number of Religious, such as
Father Humphrey Whistler, Sister Jenny and Sister Carol were to
spend time in the community, giving a breadth of churchmanship to its life and worship.

Although the Lee Abbey movement is rooted in the Anglican
tradition,[13] all three branches have always had community
members from a wide range of denominations. The overriding
concern has been that the living out of and the sharing of the
Gospel takes precedence over denominational allegiance. Of
course, this is easier in a community setting which is not a local
church (where issues such as believer's baptism and infant
baptism would soon arise).

The desire and ability to work alongside Christians of other
denominations and of different theological convictions has been
an important part of the witness of the communities. Many
community members and guests have found fresh inspiration
to work for the unity of the Church as a result of in-depth
relationships with Christians from different backgrounds.

Not only is ecumenism important because Jesus Christ prayed
for it,[14] but because we cannot afford to dissipate our efforts and
initiatives by competing with other churches. In recent years the
ecumenical movement appears to have slowed down and lost
much of its energy due, at least in part, to a weariness with
discussions about the use of church buildings, the deployment of
clergy and church structures. However, there does seem to be a
'new ecumenism' springing up from the grass-roots as local
churches work together on practical issues (employing Youth
Workers, for example) and on sharing vision for the local community. The experience of Lee Abbey is that we find unity when
we look outward from our churches and our traditions and focus
on God's mission in the world. The crying need for the Church

today is a willingness to lose ourselves for the sake of the Gospel and, in the process, to discover the Gospel anew.

An emphasis on the world

Sixth, there has been an *emphasis on the world*. From its earliest days Lee Abbey has had a European and world dimension. During the late 1940s and early 1950s the community in Devon held a series of International House-parties for people from Germany, France, Belgium, Switzerland and Holland. At times these could became very tense as people faced their anger and resentment over what had happened in the war. Much healing of relationships and memories resulted. Soon community members were being drawn from different parts of Europe, initially from the Netherlands, Denmark and Norway. At a later stage there were considerable numbers of community from Australia, New Zealand, North and South America, different countries of Africa, Japan and Korea. In more recent years there have been many community members from Eastern Europe.

The Lee Abbey International Students' Club likes to point out that the community comprises people from many different nationalities. In a different way the Lee Abbey Household communities also have an international aspect, shown most clearly in the Aston community which is set in a multi-racial part of Birmingham.

Rubbing shoulders with people from other races and cultures can be a life-changing experience as one's cultural assumptions are subtly challenged. Many Christians have gone through a time of struggle as they have gradually come to see that some of the things that they had presumed were part of the Gospel were actually cultural additions. This world dimension has been one of the most enriching aspects of the movement.

In the Diocese of Lichfield, in which I now work, we have had close working relationships with our companion dioceses in Malaysia, Canada and Maklosane. We have moved beyond the sort of exchange visits which are little more than religious tourism. Each year a number of people go overseas to share in a period of mission or ministry and we also receive teams from abroad. The first thing that happens is that our knowledge and understanding is broadened. For example, it is fascinating for British people to spend time in a culture, such as in parts of West Malaysia, where Christians are a small minority in an Islamic area. For some of the British visitors it is the first time they have met Muslims. Sharing together in God's work in a different culture can also be a profoundly converting experience. In a gently subversive way God allows us to hear the Gospel afresh, often in the casual encounters and discussions. Many people, both lay and ordained, have spent a time overseas and have had their faith shaken up and renewed.

It is an oft-repeated truism that our world is rapidly changing. Nearer to home, Lee Abbey's European community continues to develop. It has become easier for ordinary people to visit remote parts of the world, whilst television brings news of international war and conflicts into our sitting-rooms. There is an urgent need for us to build bridges if we are going to create a prosperous future. Not only are churches well placed to do this, but we have much to gain if we open ourselves up to other peoples and other cultures.

Lee Abbey and future mission

For many Christians mission and evangelism are high on the agenda. However, traditional forms of engagement are not working as well as they did in the past. In the Anglican Church much time is being spent on a recent General Synod Report entitled *Mission-Shaped Church*.[15] There is a concern in many quarters to find ways of reconnecting with the young generation, and there are many 'fresh expressions of church' emerging at grass-roots level. One of the greatest challenges for Lee Abbey is to place itself – in each of the three constituent parts, along with the Camps and the Friends – at the forefront of new missionary thinking and practice and to be a vibrant resource for the Church, as it has over the past 60 years.

NOTES

1. J. Verkuyl, *Contemporary Missiology: an introduction* (Michigan, Eerdmans, 1978), p. 1.

2. David J. Bosch, *Transforming Mission: paradigm shifts in theology of mission* (New York, Maryknoll, 1991), p. 1.

3. W. Abraham, *The Logic of Evangelism: a significant contribution to the theory and practice of evangelism* (London, Hodder & Stoughton, 1989), pp. 23–39.

4. 'More and more Christians of the old churches have come to recognize that a church which is not "the church in mission" is not church at all' – Lesslie Newbigin, *The Open Secret* (Michigan, Eerdmans, 1978), p. 2. 'God the Father sent the Son, and the Son is both the Sent One and the Sender. Together with the Father the Son sends the Holy Spirit, who in turn sends the church, congregations, apostles, and servants laying them under obligation in discharging his work' – Verkuyl, op. cit., p. 3.

5. Bosch, op. cit., pp. 10–11.

6. Quoted in Frances Young, 'Christian Attitudes to Finance in the First Four Centuries', *Epworth Review* (1977), p. 83.

7. 'We cannot get far with evangelism until three facts are faced. First, the vast majority of English people need to be converted to Christianity. Secondly, a large number of Church people also require to be converted, in the sense of their possessing that personal knowledge of Christ which can be ours only by the dedication of the whole self, whatever the cost. Thirdly, such personal knowledge of Christ is the only satisfactory basis for the testimony to others.' – *Towards the Conversion of England* (Westminster, Press and Publications Board of the Church Assembly, 1945).

8. *Evangelii Nuntiandi*, Pope Paul VI, 15.

9. However, it can also be dangerous. If it is abused it can be used to indoctrinate people – think, for example, of the Al-Qaeda training camps.

10. For example, Peter Ball, *Adult Believing: a guide to the Christian initiation of adults* (Oxford, Mowbray, 1988).

11. Quoted in Richard More, *Growing in Faith: the Lee Abbey Story* (London, Hodder & Stoughton, 1982), p. 37.

12. John Tiller, *Strategy for the Church's Ministry* (London, CIO, 1983).

13. Currently the wardens and ordained chaplains of the communities must be ordained within one of the member churches of Churches Together in Britain and Ireland. Holy Communion is usually celebrated according to Anglican rites.

14. John 17:21.

15. *Mission-Shaped Church: church planting and fresh expressions of church in a changing context* (London, Church House Publishing, 2004).